P9-AFC-220

THE
LAW (IN PLAIN ENGLISH)®
FOR
SMALL BUSINESSES

Leonard D. DuBoff

ALLWORTH PRESS
NEW YORK

Riverside Community College
Library
4800 Magnolia Avenue
Riverside, CA 92506

KF 1659 .Z9 D83 1998

DuBoff, Leonard D.

The law (in plain English)
  for small businesses

© 1998 Leonard DuBoff

All rights reserved. Copyright under Berne Copyright Convention,
Universal Copyright Convention, and Pan-American Copyright
Convention. No part of this book may be reproduced, stored in a
retrieval system, or transmitted in any form, or by any means,
electronic, mechanical, photocopying, recording, or otherwise,
without prior permission of the publisher.

Published by Allworth Press
An imprint of Allworth Communications
10 East 23rd Street, New York NY 10010

Cover design by Douglas Design Associates, New York, NY

Page composition/typography by Sharp Des!gns, Inc., Lansing, MI

ISBN: 1-880559-95-1

Library of Congress Catalog Card Number: 98-70406

To Mary Ann Crawford DuBoff,
for all you have done
and for all we have together,
and to our grandson, Brian
— welcome to our world.

Contents

Preface vii

1   Organizing Your Business 1
2   Business Organization Checklist 15
3   The Business Plan 23
4   Borrowing from Banks and Institutional Lenders 29
5   Selling Securities or Going Public 47
6   Contracts 53
7   Consignment 63
8   Collections 69
9   Expanding Your Market 79
10 Patent Law and Trade Secret Protection 87
11 Trademarks 93
12 Copyrights 107
13 Licensing 123
14 Advertising 129
15 Cyberspace 135
16 Warranty and Consumer Protection Laws 145
17 Product Liability 155
18 Business Insurance 163
19 People Who Work for You 173
20 Keeping Taxes Low 183
21 Are You Zoned to Work at Home? 203
22 Renting Commercial Space 207
23 Pension Plans as Employee Benefits 213
24 Estate Planning 221
25 How to Find a Lawyer and Accountant 233

Index 239

Preface

When I first began writing The Law (in Plain English)® series more than two and a half decades ago, my goal was to educate nonlawyers on the business aspects of their professions. At the time, I was a full-time law professor, and, as an educator, I felt that one of my missions was to provide educational tools. Later, as a full-time lawyer, I realized the importance of this series in educating my clients so that they could more effectively communicate with me. It became clear that the more knowledgeable my clients were about the myriad legal issues that they faced in their businesses and professions, the more effectively they could aid me in helping them. It is for this reason that I continue this series, and today there are In Plain English® books for writers, high-tech entrepreneurs, healthcare professionals, craftspeople, gallery operators, photographers, and this volume, for those who are involved with every aspect of small businesses.

The word "small" as used in the title is not intended to limit this text to operators of ma-and-pa operations; rather, it is intended to encompass all businesses that are not publicly traded and listed on national securities exchanges. It is likely that companies of that size would have in-house counsel trained in the various subjects discussed in this volume. However, even the principals of such companies might gain a clearer understanding of the legal issues they deal with by reading an In Plain English® book.

This book is not intended to be a substitute for the advice of a professional. Rather, it is designed to sensitize you to the issues that may require the aid of a skilled attorney or other expert. It is my sincere hope that this book will, like its predecessors in the series, be practical, useful, and readable. One of my goals in preparing this book is to enable the reader to identify problem areas and seek the aid of a skilled professional when necessary— or preferably before it becomes necessary—because it is quite common for the owners of small businesses to become embroiled in legal problems before they are able to appreciate the problem.

The law is quite complex and rapidly evolving. Since the first edition of this text was published in 1987 (a second edition was released in 1991), many changes have occurred. New business forms, such as limited liability companies and limited liability partnerships, have emerged. The World Wide Web has become a vehicle for communication and the law has been scrambling to keep pace. In writing this edition, it was my intention to chronicle the changes and convert them into a clear and understandable text that will aid the reader in understanding the current state of business law. In so doing, it is hoped that business readers will be able to more effectively communicate with their business associates and legal advisors when inevitable legal issues arise.

There are a host of individuals who have aided me in preparing this third edition of *The Law (in Plain English)® for Small Businesses*. It is impossible to identify all of them within these pages, but some deserve special recognition. I would like to thank the following friends, colleagues, former students, and associates for their valuable assistance. In particular, I would like to thank Christy O. King, associate with the law firm of DuBoff & Ross, for her aid in spearheading much of the revision work that contributed to this book. Without her attention to detail, this revision would not have been possible. I would like to thank Michael J. Supancich of the law firm of DuBoff

& Ross, who assisted with the editing and research contained in these pages. Stephen S. Staudinger of Dean Witter Reynolds, Inc., was extraordinarily helpful in providing up-to-date and accurate information about pensions and profit-sharing plans. I am also indebted to John Stevko of the accounting firm of Stevko & Miller, for his aid with the numerous changes in tax law. My colleague and former student, Emil Berg, was extremely helpful in providing recommendations with respect to the material contained in the chapter on insurance law.

A special thanks to my brother, Michael H. DuBoff of the law firm of Davidoff & Malito, and to a former student, Jason M. Cappello, Esq., for their astute comments and recommendations.

I would also like to thank everyone, and I mean everyone, at Allworth Press for their cheerful service with this book. In particular, I would like to recognize the special help of my editors, Ted Gachot and Nyier Abdou, Tad Crawford, Publisher, and my copy editor, Nancy Bernhaut.

My daughters Colleen DuBoff Haak and Sabrina DuBoff, were a tremendous aid in proofing this work and verifying much of the material that appears in this text. I am also indebted to Lynn Della and Duenna Ignacio Kawanishi for their help in proofing this manuscript. My secretaries, Peggy Reckow, Betty Scothorn, and Cheri Kraushaar deserve special recognition for their extra effort in converting my numerous interlinings and cryptic notes into a readable volume.

Finally, I would like to recognize the aid of my partner in law and in life, Mary Ann Crawford DuBoff, for all of her work on this text. Words are inadequate to express the appreciation I feel for all she has contributed to this and all of my projects.

LEONARD DuBOFF
Portland, Oregon, 1998

1

Organizing Your Business

Everyone in business knows that survival requires careful financial planning, yet few fully realize the importance of selecting the best *form* for the business. Small businesses have little need for the sophisticated organizational structures utilized in industry, but since all entrepreneurs must pay taxes, obtain loans, and expose themselves to potential liability with every sale they make, it only makes sense to structure one's business so as to minimize these concerns.

Every business has an organizational form best suited to it. When I counsel people on organizing their businesses, I usually adopt a two-step approach. First, we discuss various aspects of taxes and liability in order to decide which of the basic forms is best. There are only a handful of basic forms: the *sole proprietorship*, the *partnership*, the *corporation*, the *limited liability company*, the *limited liability partnership*, and a few hybrids. Once we have decided which of these is appropriate, we go into the organizational details such as partnership agreements, corporate bylaws, or operating agreements. These documents define the day-to-day operations of a business and, therefore, must be tailored to individual situations.

What I offer here is an explanation of the features of these kinds of organizations, including their advantages and disadvantages. This should give you an idea of which form might be best for you. I will discuss potential problems but since I cannot go into a full discussion of the more intricate details, you should consult an attorney before deciding to adopt any particular structure. My purpose is to facilitate your communication with your lawyer and to enable you to better understand the choices offered.

The American Dream: Sole Proprietorship

The technical name *sole proprietorship* may be unfamiliar to you, but chances are you are operating under this form now. The sole proprietorship is an unincorporated business owned by one person. Though not peculiar to the United States, it was, and still is, the backbone of the American dream to the extent that personal freedom follows economic freedom. As a form of business, it is elegant in its simplicity. All it requires is a little money and work. Legal requirements are few and simple. In most localities you must obtain a business license from the city or county for a small fee. If you wish to operate the business under a name other than your own, the name must be registered with the state and, in some cases, the county in which you are doing business. With these details taken care of, you are in business.

Disadvantages of Sole Proprietorship

There are many financial risks involved in operating your business as a sole proprietor. If you recognize any of these dangers as a real threat, you probably should consider an alternative form of organization.

If you are the sole proprietor of a business venture, the property you personally own is at risk. In other words, if for any reason you owe more than the dollar value of your business, your creditors can force a sale of most of your personally owned property to satisfy the debt.

For many risks, insurance is available that shifts the loss from you to an insurance company, but there are some risks for which insurance is simply not available. For instance, insurance is not generally available to protect against a large rise in the cost, or sudden unavailability of, supplies or raw materials. In addition, the cost of product liability insurance has become so high that as a practical matter it is unavailable to most businesses. Even when procured, every insurance policy has a limited, strictly defined scope of coverage. These liability risks, as well as many other uncertain economic factors, can drive a small business and its sole proprietor into bankruptcy.

Taxes for the Sole Proprietor

The sole proprietor is taxed on all profits of the business and may deduct losses. Of course, the rate of taxation will change with increases in income. Fortunately there are ways to ease this tax burden. For instance, you can establish an approved IRA or pension plan by deducting a specified amount of your net income for placement into the pension plan, an interest-bearing account, approved government securities or mutual funds, to be withdrawn later when you are in a lower tax bracket. There are severe restrictions, however, on withdrawal of this money prior to retirement age.

For further information on tax planning devices you should contact your local IRS office and ask for free pamphlets, or you might wish to use the services of an accountant experienced in dealing with business-tax planning.

Partnership

A *partnership* is defined by most state laws as an association of two or more persons to conduct, as co-owners, a business for profit. No formalities are required. In fact, in some cases people have been held to be partners even though they never had any intention of forming a partnership. For example, if you lend a friend some money to start a business, and the friend agrees to pay you a certain percentage of whatever profit is made, you may be your friend's partner in the eyes of the law even though you take no part in running the business. This is important because each partner is subject to unlimited personal liability for the debts of the partnership. Each partner is also liable for the negligence of another partner and of the partnership's employees when a negligent act occurs in the usual course of business.

This means that if you are getting involved in a partnership, you should be especially cautious in two areas. First, since the involvement of a partner increases your potential liability, you should choose a responsible partner. Second, the partnership should be adequately insured to protect both the assets of the partnership and the personal assets of each partner.

As I have already mentioned, no formalities are required to create a partnership. If the partners do not have a formal agreement defining the terms of the partnership, such as control of the partnership or the distribution of profits, state law determines the terms. State laws are based on the fundamental characteristics of the typical partnership as it has existed throughout the ages and are, therefore, thought to correspond to the reasonable expectations of the partners. The most important of these legally presumed characteristics are the following:

- No one can become a member of a partnership without the unanimous consent of all partners
- All members have an equal vote in the management of the partnership regardless of the size of their interests in it
- All partners share equally in the profits and losses of the partnership no matter how much capital they have contributed
- A simple majority vote is required for decisions in the ordinary course of business, and a unanimous vote is required to change the fundamental character of the business
- A partnership is terminable at will by any partner. A partner can withdraw from the partnership at any time, and this withdrawal will cause a dissolution of the partnership.

Most state laws contain a provision that allows the partners to make their own agreements regarding the management structure and division of profits that best suits the needs of the individual partners.

Major Items of Agreement

A comprehensive partnership agreement is no simple matter. Some major considerations in preparing a partnership agreement include the name of the partnership, a description of the business, contributions of capital by the partners, duration of the partnership, distribution of profits, management responsibilities, duties of partners, prohibited acts, and provisions for the dissolution of the partnership. (These items are detailed in chapter 2.) It is essential for potential partners to devote time and considerable care to the preparation of an agreement and to enlist the services of a business lawyer. The expense of a lawyer to help you put together an agreement suited to the needs of your partnership is usually well justified by the economic savings recouped in the smooth organization, operation, and, when necessary, the final dissolution of the partnership.

The economic advantages of doing business in a partnership form are the pooling of capital, collaboration of skills, easier access to credit enhanced by the collective credit rating, and potentially a more efficient allocation of labor and resources. A major disadvantage is that each partner is fully and personally liable for all the debts of the partnership, even if not personally involved in incurring those debts.

Taxes

A partnership does not possess any special tax advantages over a sole proprietorship. Each partner pays tax on his or her share of the profits, whether distributed or retained, and each is entitled to the same proportion of the partnership deductions and credits. The partnership must prepare an annual information return for the IRS known as Schedule K-1, Form 1065, which details each partner's share of income, credits, and deductions, and which the IRS uses to check against the individual returns filed by the partners.

The Limited Partnership

The *limited partnership* is a hybrid containing elements of both the partnership and the corporation. A limited partnership may be formed by parties who wish to invest in a business and, in return, to share in its profits, but who seek to limit their risk to the amount of their investment. The law provides such limited risk for the limited partner, but only so long as the limited partner plays no active role in the day-to-day management and operation of the business. In effect, the limited partner is very much like an investor who buys a few shares of stock in a corporation but has no significant role in running the corporation. In order to establish a limited partnership, it is necessary to have one or more general partners run the business and have full personal liability, and one or more limited partners who play a passive role.

Forming a limited partnership requires a document to be filed with the proper state office. If the document is not filed or is improperly filed, the limited partner could be treated as a general partner and thus lose the protection of limited liability. In addition, the limited partner *must* refrain from becoming involved in the day-to-day operation of the partnership. Otherwise, the limited partner might be found to be actively participating in the business, and thereby held to be a general partner with unlimited personal liability.

Limited partnership is a convenient form for securing needed financial backers who wish to share in the profits of an enterprise without undue exposure to personal liability when forming a corporation or limited liability company (LLC) may not be appropriate, e.g., when one does not meet all the requirements of an S corporation or when one does not desire ownership in an LLC. (These forms are described below.) A limited partnership can be used to attract investors when credit is hard to get or is too expensive. In return for investing, the limited partner may receive a designated share of the profits. From the entrepreneur's point of view, this may be an attractive way to fund a business since the limited partner receives nothing if there are no profits; whereas, had the entrepreneur borrowed money from a creditor, he or she would be at risk to repay the loan regardless of the success or failure of the business.

Another use of the limited partnership is to facilitate reorganization of a general partnership after the death or retirement of a general partner. Remember, a partnership can be terminated upon the request of any partner. Although the original partnership is thus technically dissolved when one partner retires, it is not uncommon for the remaining partners to agree to buy out the retiring partner's share—that is, to return that person's capital contribution and keep the business going. Raising enough cash to buy out the retiring partner, however, could jeopardize the business by forcing the remaining partners to liquidate certain partnership assets. A convenient way to avoid such a detrimental liquidation is for the retiree to step into a limited partner status. Thus, he or she can continue to share in the profits which, to some extent, flow from that partner's past labor, while removing personal assets from the risk of partnership liabilities. In the meantime, the remaining partners are afforded the opportunity to restructure the partnership funding under more favorable conditions.

What You Don't Want: Unintended Partners

Whether yours is a straightforward partnership or a limited partnership, one arrangement you want to avoid is the unintended partnership. This can occur when you work together with another person and your relationship is not described formally. For example, if you and another person decide to import, market, and sell small electronic appliances from Asia, it is essential for you to spell out in detail the arrangements between the two of you. If you do not, you could find that the other person is your partner and entitled to half the income you receive even though his or her contribution was minimal. You can avoid this by simply hiring the other person as an employee or independent contractor. Whichever arrangement you choose, you should have a detailed written agreement.

The Corporation

The word *corporation* may call to mind a vision of a large company with hundreds or thousands of employees. In fact, the vast majority of corporations in the United States are small- or moderate-sized companies. There are, of course, advantages and disadvantages to incorporating. If it appears advantageous to incorporate, you will find it can be done with surprising ease and with little expense. However, you will need a lawyer's assistance to ensure compliance with state formalities, instruction on corporate mechanics, and advice on corporate taxation.

Differences Between a Corporation and a Partnership

In describing the corporate form, it is useful to compare it to a partnership. Perhaps the most important difference is that, like limited partners, the owners of the corporation—commonly known as shareholders or stockholders—are not personally liable for the corporation's debts; they stand to lose only their investment. But unlike a limited partner, a shareholder is allowed full participation in the control of the corporation through the shareholders' voting privileges: the higher the percentage of outstanding shares owned, the more significant the control.

For the small corporation, however, limited liability may be something of an illusion because very often creditors will require that the owners personally cosign for any credit extended. In addition, individuals remain resposible for their own wrongful acts; thus, a shareholder who negligently causes an injury while engaged in corporate business has not only subjected the corporation to liability but also remains personally liable. If the other contracting party has agreed to look only to the corporation for responsibility, the corporate liability shield does, however, protect a shareholder from liability for breach of contract.

The corporate shield also offers protection in situations where an agent hired by the corporation has committed a wrongful act while working for the corporation. For example, if a management consultant negligently injures a pedestrian while driving somewhere on corporate business, the consultant will be liable for the wrongful act and the corporation *may* be liable, but the shareholder who owns the corporation will probably not be personally liable.

The second major difference between a corporation and a partnership relates to continuity of existence. The many events that can cause the dissolution of a partnership do not have the same effect on a corporation. In fact, it is common for "perpetual existence" to be established in the articles of incorporation. Shareholders, unlike partners, cannot decide to withdraw and demand a return of capital from the corporation; all they can do is sell their stock. Therefore, a corporation may have both legal and economic continuity. This can be a tremendous disadvantage to shareholders or their heirs if they want to sell stock when there are no buyers for it. However, agreements can be made that guarantee return of capital to the estate of a shareholder who dies or to a shareholder who decides to withdraw.

The third difference relates to transferability of ownership. No one can become a partner without unanimous consent of the other partners unless otherwise agreed. In a corporation, however, shareholders can generally sell all or any number of their shares to whomever they wish. If the owners of a small corporation do not want it to be open to outside ownership, transferability may be restricted by agreement of the owners.

The fourth difference is in the structure of management and control. Common shareholders are given a vote in proportion to their ownership in the corporation. Other kinds of stock can be created, with or without voting rights. A voting shareholder uses the vote to elect a board of directors and to create rules under which the board will operate.

The basic rules of the corporation are stated in its articles of incorporation that are filed with the state. These serve as the constitution for the corporation and can be amended by shareholder vote. More detailed operational rules—bylaws—should also be prepared. Both shareholders and directors may have the power to create or amend bylaws. This varies from state to state and may be determined by the shareholders themselves. The board of directors then makes operational decisions for the corporation and might delegate day-to-day control to a president.

A shareholder, even one who owns all the stock, may not preempt a decision of the board of directors. If the board has exceeded the powers granted it by the articles or bylaws, any shareholder may sue for a court order remedying the situation. If the board is within its powers, the shareholders then have no recourse except to remove the board or any board member. In a few more progressive states, a small corporation may entirely forego having a board of directors. In these cases, the corporation is authorized to allow the shareholders to vote on business decisions just as in a partnership.

The fifth distinction between a partnership and a corporation is the greater variety of means available to the corporation for raising additional capital. Partnerships are quite restricted in this regard; they can borrow money or, if all the partners agree, they can take on additional partners. A corporation, on the other hand, may issue more stock, and this stock can be of many different varieties: recallable at a set price, for example, or convertible into another kind of stock.

A means frequently used to attract a new investor is the issuance of preferred stock. The corporation agrees to pay the preferred shareholder some predetermined amount, known as a dividend preference, before it pays any dividends to other shareholders. It also means that if the corporation should go bankrupt, the preferred shareholder will generally be paid out of the proceeds of liquidation before the common shareholders, although after the corporation's creditors are paid.

In most cases, the issuance of new stock merely requires approval by a majority of the existing shareholders. In addition, corporations can borrow money on a short-term basis by issuing notes, or for a longer period by issuing debentures or bonds. Actually, a corporation's ability to raise additional capital is limited only by its lawyer's creativity and the economics of the marketplace.

The last distinction is the manner in which a corporation is taxed. Under both state and federal laws, the profits of the corporation are taxed to the corporation before they are paid out as dividends. Then, because the dividends constitute income to the shareholders, they are taxed again as the shareholder's personal income. This double taxation constitutes the major disadvantage of incorporating.

Avoiding Double Taxation of Corporate Income

There are several methods of avoiding double taxation. First, a corporation can plan its business so as not to show much profit. This can be done by drawing off what would be profit in payments to shareholders for a variety of services. For example, a shareholder can be paid a salary, rent for property leased to the corporation, or interest on a loan made to the corporation. All of these are legal deductions from the corporate income.

A corporation can also get larger deductions for the various health and retirement benefits provided for its employees than an individual or a partnership can. For example, a corporation can deduct all its payments made for an employee health plan while the employees pay no personal income tax on this benefit. Sole proprietors or partnerships, on the other hand, can deduct only a portion of these expenses.

A corporation can also reinvest its profits for reasonable business expansion. This undistributed money is not taxed as income to the individual, though the corporation must pay corporate tax on it. By contrast, the retained earnings of a partnership are taxed to the individual partners even though the money is not distributed. Corporate reinvestment has two advantages. First, the business can be built up with money that has been taxed only at the corporate level and on which no individual shareholder needs to pay any tax. Second, within reasonable limits, the corporation can delay the distribution of corporate earnings until a time of lower personal income of the shareholder and, therefore, lower personal tax rates. If, however, the amount withheld for expansion is unreasonably high, then the corporation may be exposed to a penalty. It is, therefore, wise to work with an experienced tax planner on a regular basis.

The S Corporation

Congress has created a hybrid organizational form that allows the owners of a small corporation to take advantage of many of the features described above but that is taxed in a manner similar to a partnership and can thereby avoid most of the double-taxation problems. In this form of organization, called an *S corporation*, income and losses flow directly to shareholders and the corporation pays no income tax. This form can be particularly advantageous in the early years of a corporation because the owners can deduct almost all the corporate losses from their personal incomes, which they cannot do in a standard, or C, corporation. They can have this favorable tax situation while simultaneously enjoying the corporation's limited liability status. If the corporation is likely to sustain major losses, and shareholders have other sources of income against which they wish to write off those losses, the S corporation is probably a desirable form for the business.

Small corporation as defined by the tax law does not refer to the amount of business generated; rather it refers to the number of owners. In order to qualify for S status the corporation may not have more than seventy-five owners, each of whom must be either a U.S. citizen or a certain kind of trust or nonprofit corporation. Additionally, there cannot be more than one class of stock.

Taxes

S corporations are generally taxed in the same way as partnerships, although unfortunately, the tax rules for S corporations are not as simple as those for partnerships. Generally speaking, however, the owner of an S corporation can be taxed on his or her pro rata share of the distributable profits and may deduct his or her share of distributable losses.

Limited Liability Companies

There is a relatively new business form known as the limited liability company, or LLC. This business form combines the limited liability features of a corporation with all the tax advantages available to the sole proprietor or partnerships. Although the first LLC statute was enacted in Wyoming in 1977, it did not become an attractive business form until 1988, when the Internal Revenue Service issued a ruling classifying the LLC as a partnership for tax purposes. An entrepreneur conducting business through an LLC can shield his or her personal assets from the risk of the business for all situations except the individual's own wrongful acts. This liability shield is identical to the one offered by the corporate form. The owners of an LLC can also enjoy all the tax features accorded to sole proprietors or partners in a partnership.

LLCs do not have the same restrictions imposed on S corporations regarding the number of owners, the owner's citizenship, and the type of owners (i.e., human beings or specified business forms). In fact, business corporations, partnerships, and other business forms can own interest in LLCs. LLCs may also have more than one class of ownership.

Keep in mind that the LLC form is new, so there is not yet any significant body of case law interpreting the meaning of the new statutes that created it. It is, however, extremely flexible, and in 1997 the Internal Revenue Code was amended to permit LLCs to be taxed like C corporations or like sole proprietors and partnerships. Most state LLC statutes have also been revised and now permit the organization to be run by a single manager if desired.

Limited Liability Partnerships

For businesses that have been conducted in the partnership form and desire a liability shield, the limited liability partnership or LLP is now available. This business form parallels the LLC in most respects, though it is created by converting a partnership into an LLP, and it is available for professionals who, in many states, may not conduct business through LLCs.

Licensed professionals who desire some form of liability shield may also create professional corporations. These business entities do not generally have the same liability shields available to business corporations. When LLCs were first created, most professional associations declared them analogous to business corporations and thus prohibited their use by professionals. The one profession that did permit the use of LLCs was accounting. The LLP was created as a permitted business form for all professionals.

Precautions for Minority Owners

Dissolving a corporation is not only painful because of certain tax penalties, but it is almost always impossible without the consent of the majority of the owners. This may be true of LLCs and LLPs as well. If you are involved in the formation of a corporation and will be a minority shareholder, you must realize that the majority shareholders will have ultimate and absolute control unless minority shareholders take certain precautions from the start. There are numerous horror stories relating to what some majority shareholders have done to minority shareholders. Avoiding these problems is no more difficult than drafting an agreement among the shareholders. Both LLCs and LLPs have operating agreements that can be structured for minority protection. You should always retain your own attorney to represent you during the business entity's formation, rather than waiting until it is too late.

It is important to determine which business form will be most advantageous for you. This can best be done by consulting an experienced business lawyer and having your situation evaluated. In the next chapter, I have detailed some questions that you may wish to answer before meeting with your attorney. This preparation should help minimize the amount of attorney's time necessary to create your new business entity.

2

Business Organization Checklist

As discussed in the previous chapter, there are a host of business forms available for the business entrepreneur. These forms range from the simplest—sole proprietorship—to partnerships, corporations, limited liability companies, and limited liability partnerships. The structure of your business will depend upon a number of considerations. Creating any of these business forms is a rather simple process, but to do it right and utilize all the advantages, it is highly recommended that you consult a lawyer. Of course, a lawyer's time is money, but you can save some of that money if you come properly prepared. Here is a checklist of some of the points you will need to discuss with your lawyer.

Certified Public Accountant (CPA)

Other than yourself, the most important person with whom your attorney will work is your accountant. The accountant will provide valuable input on the business's financial structure, funding, capitalization, allocation of ownership, and other issues.

Business Name

Regardless of its form, every business will have a name. Contact your attorney ahead of time with the proposed name of the business. A quick phone call or inquiry to the corporation commissioner or secretary of state will establish whether the proposed name is available. Your attorney can reserve your chosen business name until you are ready to use it. You will also have to consider whether the business will have a special mark or logo that needs federal trademark protection or state registration. For a discussion of trademarks, see chapter 11.

Business Structure: Partnership

If it is determined that you will conduct your business in the partnership form, it is essential that you have a formal, written agreement prepared by a skilled business attorney. The more time you and your prospective partners spend on being well prepared by discussing these details in advance of meeting with a lawyer, the less such a meeting is likely to cost you. The major items of a partnership agreement that you should consider are discussed below.

The Eight Basics of a Partnership Agreement

1. The Name of the Partnership

As noted above, every business will have a name. Most partnerships simply use as names the surnames of the major partners. The choice in that case is nothing more than the order of the names, which depends on various factors from prestige to the way the names sound in a particular order. If, however, the name does not include the partners' full names, it will be necessary to file the proposed business name with the state. Care should be taken to choose a name that is distinctive and not already in use. If the name is not distinctive, others can copy it; if the name is already in use, you could be liable for trade-name infringement.

2. A Description of the Business

In describing their business, the partners should agree on the basic scope of the business—its requirements in regard to capital and labor, each party's individual contributions of capital and labor, and perhaps some plans regarding future growth.

3. Partnership Capital

After determining how much capital each partner will contribute, the partners must decide when it will be contributed, how to value the property contributed, and whether a partner can contribute or withdraw any property at a later date.

4. Duration of the Partnership

Sometimes partnerships are organized for a fixed amount of time or are automatically dissolved on certain conditions, such as the completion of a project.

5. Distribution of Profits

You can make whatever arrangement you want for distribution of profits. Although ordinarily a partner does not receive a salary, it is possible to give an active partner a guaranteed salary in addition to a share of the profits. Since the partnership's profits can be determined only at the close of a business year, ordinarily distributions are not made until that time. However, it is possible to allow the partners a monthly draw of money against their final share of the profits. In some cases, it may also be necessary to allow limited expense accounts for some partners.

Not all the profits of the partnership need to be distributed at year's end. Some can be retained for expansion, an arrangement that can be provided for in the partnership agreement. Note, though, that whether or not the profits are distributed, all partners must pay tax on their shares. The tax code refers directly to the partnership agreement to determine what that share is, which shows how important a partnership agreement is.

6. Management

The power in the partnership can be divided many ways. All partners can be given an equal voice, or some more than others. A few partners might be allowed to manage the business entirely, with the remaining partners being given a vote only on specifically designated areas of concern.

Besides voting, three other areas of management should be covered. First is the question of who can sign checks, place orders, or enter into contracts on behalf of the partnership. Under state partnership laws, any partner may do these things so long as they occur in the usual course of business. But such a broad delegation of authority can lead to confusion, so it might be best to delegate this authority more narrowly. Second, it is a good idea to determine a regular date for partnership meetings. Finally, some consideration should be given to the possibility of a disagreement arising among the partners that leads to a deadlock. One way to avoid this is to distribute the voting power so as to make a deadlock impossible. In a two-person partnership, however, this would mean that one partner would be in absolute control, which might be unacceptable to the other partner. If, instead, the power is divided evenly among an even number of partners, as is often the case, the agreement should stipulate a neutral party or arbitrator who could settle any dispute and thereby avoid a dissolution of the partnership.

7. Prohibited Acts

By law, each partner owes the partnership certain duties by virtue of being an agent of the partnership. First is the duty of diligence. This means the partner must exercise reasonable care in acting as a partner. Second is a duty of obedience. The partner must obey the rules of the partnership and, most importantly, must not exceed the authority that the partnership has vested in him or her. Finally, there is a duty of loyalty. A partner may not, without approval of the other partners, compete with the partnership in another business. A partner also may not seize upon a business opportunity that would be of value to the partnership without first telling the partnership about it and allowing the partnership to pursue it, if the partnership desires. A list of prohibited acts should be made a part of the partnership agreement, elaborating and expanding on these fundamental duties.

8. Dissolution and Liquidation

A partnership is automatically dissolved upon the death, withdrawal, or expulsion of a partner. Dissolution identifies the legal end of the partnership but need not affect its economic life if the partnership agreement has provided for the continuation of the business after a dissolution. Nonetheless, a dissolution will affect the business because the partner who withdraws or is expelled, or the estate of the deceased partner, will be entitled to a return of the proportionate share of capital that the departing partner contributed. Details such as how this capital will be returned should be decided before dissolution because at the time of dissolution it may be impossible to negotiate. One method of handling this is to provide for a return of the capital in cash over a period of time. Some provision should be made so that the remaining partners will know how much of a departing partner's interest they may purchase.

After a partner leaves, the partnership may need to be reorganized and recapitalized. Again, provisions for this should be worked out in advance if possible. Finally, since it is always possible that the partners will eventually want to liquidate the partnership, it should be decided in advance who will liquidate the assets, which assets will be distributed, and what property will be returned to its original contributor.

Business Structure: Corporations, LLCs, and LLPs

There are usually two reasons for creating a business form such as a corporation, LLC, or LLP: limiting personal liability and minimizing income tax liability. The second reason is generally applicable to a business that is earning a good deal of money. Even if you are not in that category, you may nevertheless want to consider creating a business identity in order to limit your personal liability. Corporations, LLCs, and LLPs are hypothetical legal "persons" and, as such, are responsible for their own acts and contracts. Thus, if a consumer in a retail store slips on a banana peel, if a consultant's car negligently injures a pedestrian, or if the food your restaurant served causes food poisoning, the corporation, LLC, or LLP, not its owners, will be liable, assuming the proper formalities have been adhered to. It should be noted that any individual personally responsible for a wrongful act will also be liable.

Officers and Structure

Who will be president, vice president, secretary, and treasurer? In the case of the LLCs or LLPs electing centralized management, who will the manager be? It may be that the corporate bylaws or the LLP's or LLC's management agreement should have a separate description for specialized officers.

State statutes generally require a corporation, LLC, or LLP to have some chief operating officer such as a president. In addition, state statutes may require other administrative officers such as a secretary.

Owners

How many shares should your corporation be authorized to issue? In the case of LLCs and LLPs, certificates of participation, which resemble shares of stock in a corporation, are used and the same considerations for their issuance are present. How many units should be issued when the business commences operations, and how many should be held in reserve for future issuance? Should there be separate classes of corporate shareholders and LLC or LLP owners?

If the corporation or LLC is to be family owned, ownership may be used to some extent as a means of estate planning. Therefore, you might also wish to ask your attorney about updating your will at the same time you incorporate or create an LLC. While LLPs may be used for this purpose, it is not as common.

Owner Agreements

If your corporation has several shareholders, or if the LLC or LLP has several owners, has a method been established to prevent an owners' voting deadlock? You may also wish to discuss with your lawyer the possibility of creating owner agreements that govern employment status of key individuals or commit owners to voting a certain way on specific issues.

The Buy-Sell Agreement

The first meeting with your lawyer is a good time to discuss buy-sell agreements. What happens when one of the owners wishes to leave the business? Under what circumstances should he or she be able to sell to outsiders? In closely held corporations, the corporation or other shareholders are generally granted the first option to buy the stock; the law requires a restriction on transferability of ownership. What circumstances should trigger the corporation's or other shareholders' right to buy the stock—death, disability, retirement, termination, and so forth? Should the buy-sell agreement be tied to key-person insurance that would fund the purchase of ownership interest by the corporation, LLC, or LLP in the event of a key owner's death? What will be the mechanism for valuing stock, LLC, or LLP interest—annual appraisal, book value, multiple earnings, arbitration, or some other method?

Planning for Future Owners

Are there plans to take on new investors, shareholders, or certificate owners in the future? Do you have plans for converting the corporation into one that is publicly held, that is, owned by a large number of investors? If so, the initial structure of the articles of incorporation and stock may be used as an important planning tool for the future. While ownership interests in LLCs or LLPs cannot be publicly traded, it is still possible to bring in some additional owners. If this is anticipated, you and your attorney should discuss the method by which this may be accomplished and the legal restrictions that are imposed on the sale and transfer of LLC or LLP interests.

Capitalization

At this point, the attorney works closely with your CPA. What will be the initial capitalization or funding of the corporation, LLC, or LLP? Will owners make loans to the business and contribute the rest in exchange for ownership interest? What is being contributed by owners in exchange for their interests—money, past services, equipment, assets of an ongoing business, licensing agreements, or other things? What value will be placed on assets that are contributed to the corporation, LLC, or LLP?

The Board of Directors

Who will be on the board of directors? How many initial directors will there be? (It is a good idea for there to be an odd number of directors in order to avoid the potential for a voting deadlock.) Will owners have the right to elect members of the board of directors based on their percentages of ownership?

Housekeeping

Your attorney will need to know several other details. For instance, the number of employees the business anticipates for the coming twelve-month period must be stated on the application for a federal tax ID number. Will the business's tax year end on December 31 or on another date? Will the business's accounting be on a cash basis or accrual basis? Will the business authorize salaries for its officers? What will be the date for the annual meeting of the board of directors and owners? Who will be the registered agent? Generally, your attorney will assume this role. Which bank will your business use?

Employee Benefits

Be prepared to consider employee benefit plans such as life and health insurance, profit sharing, pension or other retirement plans, employee ownership programs, as well as other fringe benefits. Even if you do not plan to implement such programs when the corporation, LLC, or LLP is created, it is nonetheless a good idea to consider whether such programs may be instituted in the future.

S or C Corporation, or LLC or LLP?

Will the corporation elect to be an S corporation, where income and most losses flow directly to shareholders, and the corporation pays no income tax? Will it be a standard C corporation, which does pay income tax and where corporate income is not taxed to the shareholders? If the corporation is likely to sustain major losses, and shareholders have other sources of income against which they wish to write off those losses, chances are the S election would be appropriate.

Like S corporations, neither LLCs nor LLPs are taxable entities although the pass-through of profits and losses in an LLC or LLP, as distinguished from an S corporation, is actually more analogous to the tax treatment accorded partnerships.

As you can see, there is much to discuss at the first meeting with your lawyer. A little time and thought prior to that meeting will prove to be a worthwhile investment.

3

The Business Plan

Every business needs capital at one time or another. This funding might be sought as bank loans, other conventional forms of financing, or as venture capital. It might also be obtained through a public sale of securities, which is discussed in chapter 5. No matter what the source of financing, an important first step is the preparation of a business plan. This can aid a banker, venture capitalist, or prospective owner in evaluating your company. A business plan may be considered a road map to determine the course your business will travel from start-up to full operation.

The structure and content of your business plan will vary depending upon such factors as the company's stage of development, the nature of the business, and the type of markets it will serve. There are a host of different formats that have been used for business plans. Although the order of presentation is by no means standard, each of the following topics should be addressed in structuring any business plan.

Executive Summary

This section of the plan provides the reader with a short overview of the key elements of the business plan. Since sophisticated businesspeople are turned away by exaggeration, the summary must provide an accurate appraisal of your business while distinguishing your product or service and organization from others that are competing in the same market. The summary should also describe your management team, emphasizing experience and skills, but should not ignore management weaknesses and how you expect to overcome them. Another important part of the summary will be your key financial projections and funding requirements to meet those projections. Above all, the summary must be designed to catch the reader's attention. Unless the summary inspires one to read further, it has not served its purpose.

History

Businesspeople want to know about a business's past performance before they assess its future potential. Toward this end, the business plan should provide a brief history of the business, including (1) when it was founded, (2) subsequent development and growth, (3) how it has been organized (for example, as a partnership, corporation, LLC, or LLP), and (4) how well past performance reflects future potential. If you have good reason to believe that the business's past performance is not indicative of future potential, be sure to state those reasons in this section.

Products and Services

This section describes in detail the products and services of your business, including a summary explaining any unique features and a statement about performance and present status, and any special services provided such as newsletters or catalogs. Keep in mind, however, that investors are not likely to have expertise with your business. This section should be written in language that is easily understood by businesspeople with nontechnical backgrounds.

The Market

This section should contain a comprehensive description of the market your business intends to target. If the product or service you are selling is particularly innovative, such as Web site development, independent market research may need to be included to define both the initial and future markets. If the product or service you are involved with has been available for some time, the market has most likely already been defined. In that case, you may be able to rely on available data from similar businesses, industry professional associations, the Small Business Administration, chambers of commerce, or the like.

For purposes of obtaining investment capital, the market section may be the most important part of your business plan. To the banker, venture capitalist, or prospective owner, a business without a strong understanding of the targeted market is a bad risk, even if the work to be sold is first-rate. Consequently, the market description should be more detailed than the product or service description. This will indicate to potential investors that you understand the priority of market over product or service.

The Competition

Identify your competitors, discuss their relative strengths and weaknesses, and indicate the market share likely held by each. Include a forecast of the market share you expect to capture in the first three to five years, and the sources from which you expect to draw customers. Be sure to spell out your rationale for each projection—more innovative products or creative promotion, marketing, favorable reviews, price, service, or other factors. As with all projections in the business plan, do not understate the strengths of your competition while overstating your own. Sophisticated businesspeople will not back a company that does not have a realistic view of its competition.

Source of Work

Obtaining sought-after products or services at an economical price and having the ability to sell the work or provide the service expeditiously are the key to profit making. This section should discuss the trade shows that you attend, detail your suppliers, and identify those with whom you have exclusivity agreements. Additionally, you should explain the steps taken by you to expand your product or service line, as well as the markets for it, and whether you acquire products at wholesale or on consignment. In some businesses, such as those selling vehicles, it would be appropriate to discuss whether you handle resales, rebuilts, or only newly manufactured vehicles. You should also present information about the reputation of the product including, for example, favorable reviews and relevant data from recognized publications such as *Consumer Reports* or *Money* magazine.

Management

As a general rule, bankers, venture capitalists, and prospective owners would favor investing in a start-up business with first-rate management over an established business with mediocre management. This priority should be reflected in your business plan.

In this section, emphasize the experience of each key management executive. Include job descriptions and salaries, and provide résumés detailing each executive's past business experience, education, publications, and any other information that will indicate to potential financiers that you have a qualified management team. If your current management team has weak spots, define them and explain how they will be corrected.

Financial Data

Superior products or services and top-flight management count for nothing if your financial projects do not allow for a substantial return on investment. Consequently, this section is the bottom line of your business plan. Begin by summarizing previous financial performance. If your business is new, be sure that all financial projections are realistic and justifiable. Remember that most prospective investors and lenders are sophisticated and will check out other comparable businesses. If your projections deviate widely from the industry norm, you will lose both the credibility and the financing you seek. Furthermore, do not inundate your reader with yards of computer-generated spreadsheets. Your financial data should be concise and easy to understand.

Finally, your financial section should discuss the financing itself. Indicate how much money the business needs, the form of financing sought, and how the money is to be used. Most important, discuss the projected return within the next five years of operation. As with all financial information, be realistic and support your projections with solid data and a sound rationale.

The Business-Plan Team

The development of a well-written business plan requires considerable undertaking. It forces you to focus your ideas, ferret out weak spots in your organization, and turn abstract concepts into concrete plans. Experienced professionals such as lawyers and accountants can provide invaluable assistance in putting together a sound and attractive business plan. Your lawyer can help your business obtain the legal protection that it needs while steering you away from the legal pitfalls that face all new or expanding businesses. Your CPA can assist you with the myriad financial assessments you must make. A knowledgeable and respected lawyer and accountant can lend credibility to your numbers and projections. Beyond this, experienced lawyers and accountants have invaluable contacts within the venture-capital and banking communities. They can tell you who has the capital, where it is being invested, and how you can best get a share. By enlisting the help of experienced professionals and following the suggestions presented here, you can develop a business plan that will help you attract the financing you need for your new or expanding business. In addition, fashioning a business plan will cause you to formulate a program that you will likely find useful in focusing your energy so that you can realize your business objectives.

4

Borrowing from Banks and Institutional Lenders

Commercial loans can be a valuable source of needed capital for qualified business borrowers. While some entrepreneurs are able to attract venture capital, this is uncommon for most small businesses since venture capitalists typically expect a potential return of between four to six times their risk capital within a comparatively short period of time, as well as some form of ownership position in the borrower's business. It is essential to work with an experienced business lawyer when dealing with venture capitalists since these arrangements are typically hammered out on a case-by-case basis. It has been said that the golden rule in dealing with venture capitalists is, "the one who has the gold is the one who makes the rules."

Small businesses sometimes seek loans from institutional lenders, such as credit unions, insurance companies, and pension trusts. Most institutional lenders follow the same procedures as banks and demand the same type of information. Unfortunately, institutional lenders other than banks will rarely deal with small businesses, particularly when the potential borrower does not have an extensive track record. It is for this reason that I will focus on bank lending, though you should consider these other sources of funds when seeking a loan.

Lending policies vary dramatically from institution to institution. You should, therefore, talk to several banks to determine which might be likely to lend to your business and which have the most favorable loan terms. While lenders, by nature, are conservative in their lending policies, you may discover some to be more flexible than others. To save time and increase the chances of loan approval, it makes sense to first approach those banks that are most likely to view your proposal favorably and whose lending criteria you feel you can meet.

You should not limit your search for a loan to your community. A state-wide, regional, or even national search may be necessary before you find the right combination of willing lender and favorable terms. Using your credit card as a source of financing is not a good idea except in the most extreme cases. Interest rates are high and the terms are generally not good for business planning.

After having shopped the marketplace and decided on a particular bank, you will be ready for the next step—preparing the loan proposal. The importance of being properly prepared before taking this critical step cannot be overemphasized. Loan officers are not likely to be impressed by a hastily prepared application containing vague, incomplete information and unsubstantiated claims. Many loan requests are doomed at this early stage because ill-prepared applicants failed to adequately present themselves and their businesses to the lender even though the proposed ventures are in fact sound. What, then, should a borrower understand about the lending process?

The Loan Proposal

Inexperience with the bank's lending procedures can result in an unexpected rejection. Knowing the bank's lending policy and following its procedure is, therefore, essential. Just what does a lender look for in a loan application? At a minimum, a borrower should be prepared to satisfactorily address each of the following questions:

- Is your business "creditworthy"?

- For what purpose is the money needed?
- Do you need a short- or long-term loan?
- How much money do you really need?
- What kind of collateral do you and your business have to secure the loan?

The lender's decision to grant or refuse the loan request will be based on your answers to these questions.

Is Your Business Creditworthy?

The ability to obtain money when you need it may be as important to the operation of your business as having a good location and the right equipment. But before an institution will agree to lend you money, the loan officer must be satisfied that you and your business constitute a good risk—that is, that you are creditworthy. This decision includes several considerations.

Good Character

The lender will want to know what sort of person you are. Do you have a good reputation in the community and in your industry? Are you known in the community? What is your past credit history, and what is the likelihood that you will repay the loan if your business falters or even fails?

Despite its subjective nature, this character factor figures prominently in the lender's decisionmaking. It is not uncommon for a loan officer to deny a loan request irrespective of the applicant's qualifications on paper if the officer is not convinced of the borrower's good character. Even for "signature loans"—which require only the applicant's signature and are available only to businesses and entrepreneurs with the highest credit standing, business integrity, and management skills—the applicant's character will affect the institution's decision to make a loan.

Is the Cushion on the Loan Large Enough?

The lender will want to know if the borrower has included a suitable allowance for unexpected business developments in the loan request. That is, does the loan proposal realistically allow for the vicissitudes of operating a business and provide for alternative resources to meet the borrower's obligation if the business expectations are not met, or is the borrower stretching to the limit, leaving no margin for error so that repayment can be made only if the proposed venture is successful? In the latter circumstance, the lender may consider the loan too risky.

For What Purpose Is the Money Needed?

Is the money needed to purchase inventory? Or to acquire fixed assets, such as machinery or equipment? The answer to this question will determine what type of loan—long- or short-term—the applicant should request. Loans needed to purchase inventory, especially where the applicant's business is highly seasonal, will generally be short-term loans requiring repayment within one year or less. This is because the bank will likely anticipate repayment from the sale of the assets financed by the loan.

Intermediate-term loans, which require payment between one and five years, and long-term loans, which extend payments over ten or even fifteen years, are more appropriate for purchases of fixed assets since repayment is expected to be made not from the sale of these assets but from the earnings generated by the company's ongoing use of them. Those assets produce income at a much slower rate, hence the bank's willingness to allow repayment over a longer period. Bear in mind that commercial lenders are interested in offering funds to successful businesses in need of additional capital to expand and increase profitability. They are not particularly inclined to make loans to businesses needing the money to pay off existing debts.

When and How Will the Loan Be Repaid?

When and how the loan will be repaid is closely associated with the questions of how much money is needed and for what purpose. The banker will use judgment and professional experience to assess your business ability and the likelihood of your future success. The banker will want to know whether or not the proposed use of the borrowed funds justifies the repayment schedule requested. As the borrower, you *must* be able to demonstrate that the cash flow anticipated from the proceeds of the loan will be adequate to meet the repayment terms if the loan is granted.

The Business Outlook

The lender will be evaluating the business outlook, for your company in particular and for your type of business in general, in light of contemporary economic realities. Can your proposed use of the loan be reasonably expected to produce the anticipated increased revenues for your business? While your proposed plan may appear viable on paper, it may not be realistic given the state of the economy within which your company operates.

Financial Evidence

Remember that bankers prefer to make loans to solvent, profitable, growing enterprises. They seek assurance that the loan will contribute to that growth since your repayment ability is directly related to your success. As noted previously, bankers are not interested in lending money so that a business can pay off already existing loans. To aid the bank in understanding the financial health of your business, you probably will be asked to provide specific financial data. Two basic financial documents are customarily submitted for this purpose: the balance sheet and the profit and loss statement. The balance sheet will aid the bank in evaluating your business's viability, while the profit and loss statement summarizes the business's current performance. Unless yours is a new venture, you should be prepared to submit these financial reports for at least the past two or three years, since they are the principal means for measuring your company's stability and growth potential. Ideally, an independent CPA will have prepared these statements.

Analyzing Your Business Potential

In interviewing loan applicants and in studying the financial records of their businesses, the bank is especially interested in the following facts and figures:

General Information

Are the company books and financial records up-to-date, accurate, and in good condition, or are they incomplete, infrequently maintained, and in disarray? Haphazard recordkeeping not only fails to reflect the business's true financial state, but demonstrates poor managerial skills. For obvious reasons, banks are reluctant to back poorly run businesses, viewing them as too risky.

The lender will also be interested in the current condition of your business accounts payable and notes payable. Are those obligations being paid in a timely fashion or are they overdue? If you are not presently able to meet existing debts, the lender will be hard-pressed to understand how you expect to be able to meet any additional obligations. Perhaps the requested funds will solve cash-flow problems you now have and will also increase earnings so that you will be able to bring past-due accounts current while adequately handling the added debt. In this situation, you might overcome the lender's skepticism by presenting a well-thought-out, solid business plan that clearly demonstrates how the new loan will solve, rather than add to, the business's financial problems and will boost revenues.

Additionally, the lender will likely want to know the salaries of the owner/manager and other company officers to see if they are reasonable. Excessive salaries represent an unacceptable drain on company resources and profits, which may adversely affect the company's ability to meet debt obligations.

The lender will also be interested in the size of your work force. Does it seem adequate to maximize the business's potential, or does it seem excessive compared to other, similar businesses?

You should be prepared to discuss the adequacy of your company's insurance coverage, your present tax situation (whether all taxes are current), and if your business sells a product, the size, if any, of your order backlog.

All these factors say something about the financial state of your business. Although the lender may inquire into other areas, the borrower who knows the type of general information of interest to a lender and can present it articulately greatly increases the chances of having the loan approved.

Accounts Receivable

Of particular interest to the bank will be the number of customers that are behind in their payments to you, and how far behind they are. The lender will also want to know what percent of your company's total accounts receivable are owed by customers that are currently behind in their payments as well as whether a major account is behind, in which event the bank will want to know the likelihood of this account eventually being paid. The accounts receivable situation is of special interest to a lender when the borrower is relying on those accounts to provide the cash flow needed to service the requested loan.

You should also expect the potential lender to ask if your business has an adequate cash reserve to cover questionable accounts, and whether the accounts receivable have already been pledged as collateral. A lender who secures a loan with collateral that has already been pledged to a prior lender will, in most cases, be limited in its ability to foreclose on that collateral if the debtor defaults. The prior lender has first right to liquidate the collateral while subsequent lenders will receive only those proceeds remaining after the prior debt is fully satisfied.

Inventory

If the applicant's business involves the sale of goods, the bank will need to know the state of the current inventory. Is it in good shape or will it have to be marked down prior to sale? Is the inventory raw materials or the finished product? Banks are interested in unpledged inventory as a possible source of collateral and also as a source of future revenues. The bank may also be interested in the inventory turnover rate, which reflects the demand for your product and aids in evaluating the accuracy of your revenue projections.

Fixed Assets

Since fixed assets can be used to secure the loan, the bank will likely be interested in the type, condition, age, and current market value of your company's equipment, machinery, etc. You should be prepared to explain how these assets have been depreciated, their useful life expectancy, and whether they have been previously mortgaged or pledged as collateral to another lender. In addition, be ready to discuss any need or plans to acquire fixed assets. On the one hand, this need could mean additional debt obligations in the near future; on the other hand, it could explain and justify your projected growth.

Options for Owners of New Businesses

This analysis applies primarily to loan requests made by established, proven businesses. New business–loan applicants will probably not be able to supply much of the information described here. While this will not necessarily preclude having a loan approved, it could make its approval more difficult. You should be aware that new-business loans constitute only approximately 5 percent of all business loans made.

This reluctance to finance unproven businesses, understandably frustrating to new-business owners, is consistent with the traditionally conservative nature of banks, which owe a fiduciary duty to their stockholders and depositors to disburse funds in a prudent, responsible manner. In light of the extraordinarily high failure rate of new businesses, compounded by the fact that a new business generally cannot provide adequate financial data to evaluate its potential for success, the lender is hard-pressed to justify making high-risk loans. Even where the new-business borrower offers more than adequate collateral to secure the loan, the request may be denied.

Banks are comfortable lending money and earning profits from the interest charged on their loans. They are not comfortable in the role of an involuntary partner in the failing business of a delinquent debtor. Even though banks secure loans with a wide range of collateral, they understandably are not anxious to have to foreclose on that security. They are not in the business of selling business machinery or inventory, or of trying to collect a delinquent debtor's accounts receivable. Although banks try to protect themselves by lending only a fraction of the collateral's market value, they still may not obtain the full amount that they are owed in a "distress sale" of that collateral since this type of sale traditionally attracts bargain-hunters who will often buy only at prices well below true market value. With an understanding of these dynamics, a new business–loan applicant can better appreciate a bank's hesitation in approving a loan.

Banks do make some loans to new businesses. The entrepreneur will need to demonstrate a good reputation for paying debts and to offer evidence of business management skills. Perhaps you have firsthand knowledge and expertise in the type of business you propose to establish as a result of having been previously employed in the same or a closely related field. If so, emphasize that. In addition, provide a sound business plan to support your projections. You can further improve your chances of obtaining a loan if you have invested your own money in the business, thus indicating your confidence in its success. If possible, show that the business has a good debt-equity ratio, and that it is not saddled with an inordinately high debt.

Even if your loan is initially refused, it is important to establish a good working relationship with a bank. Any initial business success will impress upon the bank the soundness of your plan, thereby opening the door for future financing should the need arise.

Short- or Long-Term Financing?

Once the bank has evaluated the creditworthiness of your business, you should be ready to explain the appropriateness of the kind of loan requested. I briefly mentioned this topic above, but it deserves some additional attention. It is important to be able to convince the lender that your proposed use of the borrowed money will generate the additional revenue needed to pay the loan during the repayment period. Short-term loans are appropriate for purchasing inventory or facilitating collection of outstanding accounts receivable. They are expected to be repaid as the inventory is sold or as the accounts are collected. Long-term loans are customarily used to finance acquisition of fixed assets, which, though they may produce slow earnings initially, are expected to increase earnings in the long run. Depending upon your credit reputation, short-term loans may be available with or without security. It is more likely that long-term loans will require adequate security and necessitate a pledge of personal, as well as business, assets.

How Much Money Will You Need?

The lender is also concerned about the amount of the loan being adequate since an undercapitalized business is more likely to get into financial trouble. Similarly, a lender will be reluctant to approve a loan that is excessive since the debt service may result in an unnecessarily high cash drain on the company. The loan should net the borrower the amount necessary to accomplish the desired goal with a slight cushion for error and no more.

Estimating the amounts needed to finance building construction, conversion, or expansion—long-term loans—is relatively easy, as is estimating the cost of fixed-asset acquisition. On the other hand, working-capital needs—short-term loans—are more difficult to assess and depend upon the type of business. To plan your working-capital requirements, it is important to know the cash flow of your business, present and anticipated. This simply involves a projection of all the elements of cash receipts and disbursements at the time they are likely to occur. These figures should be projected monthly to aid the bank in its evaluation.

What Hind of Collateral Do Lenders Require?

Sometimes loans will be made solely on the borrower's signature. More frequently, banks will require collateral to secure the loan. Acceptable collateral can take a variety of forms. The type and amount of collateral necessary in a given situation will depend on the particular bank's lending policies and the borrower's financial state. In general, banks will accept the following types of collateral as security for a business loan:

Endorsers', Co-makers', or Guarantors' Promises to Pay

You may have to get other people to sign a note in order to bolster your credit. These people—sureties—may cosign your note as endorsers, comakers, or guarantors. While the law makes some subtle distinctions as to when each of these sureties becomes liable for the borrower's debt, in essence these parties will be expected to pay back the borrowed funds if the borrower fails to do so. The bank may or may not require sureties to pledge their own assets as security for their promise to pay upon the borrower's default. This will depend to a great extent on the surety's own financial situation.

Assignment of Leases

Assigning a lease as a form of security is particularly appropriate for franchise situations. If the bank lends a business franchise money for a building and takes back a mortgage, that mortgage may be secured by assigning to the lender the lease entered into between the franchiser and the franchisee that will occupy the building. If the franchiser fails to meet mortgage payments, the bank can directly receive the franchisee's lease payments in satisfaction of the franchiser's debt.

Warehouse Receipts

Banks will accept commodities as security by lending money on a warehouse receipt. Such a receipt is usually delivered directly to the bank and shows that the merchandise used as security either has been placed in a public warehouse or has been left on your premises under the control of a bonded employee. Such loans are generally made only on standard, readily marketable goods.

Security Interests

Equipment loans may be secured by giving the bank a lien on the equipment you are buying. The amount loaned will likely be less than the purchase price. How much less will be determined by the present and future market value of the equipment and its rate of depreciation. You will be expected to adequately insure the equipment, to properly maintain it, and to protect it from damage.

Real Estate Holdings

You may be able to borrow against the equity in your personal real estate holdings as well as those of the business. Again, you will likely be required to maintain the property in good condition and carry adequate insurance on the property for the benefit of the lender at least up to the amount of the loan.

Accounts Receivable

Many banks will lend money secured by your business's accounts receivable. In effect, the bank is relying on your customers to pay off your obligation to the bank.

Savings Accounts and Life Insurance Policies

Sometimes you may get a loan by assigning your savings account to the lender. The lender will then keep your passbook while notifying the savings account holder of the existence of the debt in order to ensure that the account will not be diminished during the term of the loan. Loans can also be made up to the cash value of a life insurance policy, but you must be prepared to assign the policy over to the lender.

Stocks and Bonds

Stocks and bonds may be accepted as collateral for a loan if they are readily marketable. However, banks will typically lend no more than 75 percent of the market value of a high-grade security. If the value of the securities drops below the lender's required margin, the borrower may be asked to provide additional security for the loan.

Inventory

As discussed above, business inventory, either on hand or to be acquired in the future, can be used as security for short-term loans. The lender will expect the loan to be repaid from the revenues generated by the sale of this inventory on a timely basis. Inventory may also be used as collateral for long-term loans when the lender establishes what is called a *field warehousing* arrangement. In this situation, the inventory is segregated and identified as collateral for a loan, and an employee responsible to the lender is placed in charge of the field warehouse.

Intellectual Property

Patents, copyrights, trademarks, and other forms of intellectual property may be used as collateral for a loan. There is an increasing body of case law surrounding the methods by which these assets are to be secured. Unfortunately, many lenders are unfamiliar with methods of valuing the potential worth of intellectual properties and, thus, may not be willing to attribute a meaningful value to them. If you plan to pledge your intellectual property as security for a loan, it would be beneficial for you to attempt to first obtain an appraisal of it.

Lender's Rules and Limitations

Once the loan has been approved in principal, it is likely that the bank will impose certain rules and constraints on you and your business. These serve to protect the lender against unnecessary risk and against the possibility of your engaging in poor management practices. You, your attorney, and your business advisor should evaluate all the terms and conditions of the loan in order to determine whether it is acceptable. If the bank's requirements are too onerous, it may be appropriate for you to decline this loan and seek alternative financing. Never agree to restrictions to which you cannot realistically adhere. On the other hand, if the terms and conditions of the loan are acceptable even though they are demanding, it may be appropriate to take the loan. In fact, some borrowers view these limitations as an opportunity for improving their own management techniques and business profitability.

Especially when making long-term loans, the lender will be interested in the net earning power of the borrowing company, the capability of its management, the long-range prospects of the company, and the long-range prospects of the industry of which the company is a part.

As a result of the bank's scrutiny of your company, the kinds of limitations imposed will depend to a great extent on the company itself. If the company is a good risk, only minimum limitations need be set. A poor risk, of course, should expect greater limitations to be placed on it. Three common types of limitations you are likely to encounter are repayment terms, use of pledged security, and periodic reporting.

Repayment Terms

The bank will want to set a loan-repayment schedule that accurately reflects your ability to earn revenues sufficient to meet the proposed obligation. Risky businesses can expect shorter terms, while proven enterprises may receive longer periods within which to repay the loan.

Use of Pledged Security

Once a lender agrees to accept collateral to secure a loan, it will understandably be keenly interested in assuring that, should the need arise, the collateral will still be available to satisfy the debt. To this end, the lender may take actual possession of the collateral if it is stocks, bonds, or other negotiable instruments. Of course a bank is not likely to take physical possession of a business's inventory or fixed assets and remove them to the bank's vault.

There are, however, other ways a bank can obtain possession of your fixed assets while allowing you to use them. For example, the lender could "perfect"—legally establish—a *security interest* in machinery and intellectual property, as well as equipment used in your plant or business by filing a financing statement in the appropriate state or county office. (A security interest is the legal term for a lender's rights in collateral.) Real estate mortgages are perfected by having them recorded in the appropriate government offices, and security interests in inventory can be perfected for most purposes by either filing a financing statement or establishing a field warehousing system, or both. In these situations, the bank may impose restrictions on the use of the collateral and require that it be properly maintained and adequately insured. The bank may further limit or prohibit you from pledging the same collateral for any other business debts or loans.

While this sounds reasonable, you should recognize that such restrictions may seriously hamper your ability to borrow additional funds should the need arise. For example, where inventory is used as collateral, you must find out exactly how much of your inventory is involved. A bank may ask for only a percentage of the total inventory to secure the loan. More likely, though, the bank's security interest will extend to the company's entire inventory on hand at any given time, as well as any later acquired inventory. Here lies the potential problem. The inventory's value may well exceed the amount of the loan that it secures. Nonetheless, you may find yourself in the position of not being able to use any of the inventory as collateral for additional loans. In cases where this situation is likely to arise, you are well advised to consider alternative sources of collateral.

Periodic Reporting

To protect itself, a lender may require you to supply it with certain financial statements on a regular basis, perhaps quarterly or even monthly. From these, the lender can see if in fact the business is performing up to the expectations projected in the loan application. This type of oversight serves not only to reassure the lender that the loan will be repaid, but also to identify and help solve problems early on before they become insurmountable and threaten the business's viability.

Details of the Agreement

The loan agreement itself is a tailor-made document—a contract between the lender and borrower—that spells out in detail all the terms and conditions of the loan. The actual restrictions placed on the loan will be found in the agreement under a section entitled "Covenants." Negative covenants are things that you may not do without the lender's prior approval such as incurring additional debt or pledging the loan's collateral or other business assets to another lender as collateral for a second loan. On the other hand, positive covenants spell out those things that you must do, such as carry adequate insurance, provide specified financial reports, and repay the loan according to the terms of the loan agreement. Note that with the lender's prior consent the terms and conditions contained in the loan agreement can be amended, adjusted, or even waived. Remember that you can negotiate the loan terms with the lender before signing. True, the bank is in the superior position, but legitimate lenders are happy to cooperate with qualified borrowers.

The Loan Application

Having targeted the source for funds and having analyzed the business in terms you now know lenders look at, you are ready to develop the loan request. Though most lenders will require the application to include the same standard, essential information, they often differ as to the proper format of the application. Some lenders may provide suggested formats; others may require a specific format. The actual content, length, and formality will depend on the lender's familiarity with your business, the amount of money requested, and the proposed use of the borrowed funds. A simple application form and a conversation may be adequate for your local banker. The start-up business seeking substantial funds from lenders unfamiliar with it will be required to provide much more extensive documentation, including a detailed plan of the entire business.

The business loan applicant is typically asked to submit any or all of the following information:

- *Personal financial statements* These indicate the applicant's personal net worth. This is helpful in evaluating creditworthiness and revealing potential sources of collateral as well as estimating repayment capabilities.

- *Recent and current tax filings* These should include filings of the individual and of the business.
- *The business's financial statements* As mentioned above, these ideally should extend back for at least two or three years and should have been prepared and authenticated by an independent CPA. The lender may also request cash-flow statements and profit projections.
- *A business history* This should include past profit or loss patterns, current debt-to-equity ratio, current and projected cash flow, and present and projected future earnings.
- *A business plan* This should explain the proposed use of the requested funds and how the loan will benefit the business. The length and content of this plan will vary according to the financial health of the applicant's business and the amount and type of loan applied for.

Other documentation may also be requested. The individual lender will indicate what is needed in light of the given circumstances.

Importance of Communication When Problems Arise

Once a loan is approved and disbursed, the borrower must address a new set of obligations and liabilities. Of course, if all goes according to plan, the loan proceeds are invested, the business prospers, the loan is repaid on schedule, and all parties live happily ever after. However, the business world is fraught with uncertainty. If the business falters and revenues tumble, the borrower may not be able to meet the debt obligations. In this unfortunate event, it becomes imperative that the borrower reacts responsibly, choosing to view the lender as a potential ally in solving problems rather than as an adversary. At least initially, banks are not eager to exercise their right to foreclose on the collateral securing the loan at the first indication that the debt may not be repaid. They likely have no experience in marketing the types of collateral involved, nor do they want to run a distress sale, which, at best, would probably bring in only a fraction of the money owed. Additionally, foreclosing against the business's assets further decreases the bank's chance of recovering any of the unpaid balance since the borrower, having been stripped of the means to carry on the business, is likely to be insolvent and facing bankruptcy. Even if the lender can liquidate the collateral at its current fair market value, that value may be well below the value agreed upon when the loan was made. For these and other reasons, banks foreclose on collateral only as a last resort.

Bear in mind that, in general, lenders prefer to work with a potentially defaulting debtor to help ease the debt burden so that the borrower can overcome the problems, stay in business, and reestablish the enterprise's profitability. To this end, lenders through their experiences have learned to identify a variety of red flags as indications that the debtor is experiencing financial difficulty. For example, the alert is sounded when loan payments start to be made later and later each month, or when the business's account increasingly shows checks being dishonored for insufficient funds.

When the lender sees these signals, the account may be assigned to a separate department set up within the bank to assist borrowers in overcoming problems. The bank may be willing to offer a variety of accommodations to help the borrower. Repayment terms can be extended, the amount of payment due each month can be temporarily reduced, or the bank may accept repayment of interest only until the business has overcome its temporary difficulties. The bank may be in a position to offer advice for ways to help solve the business's problems, particularly if poor management is the source of the difficulties.

How far and to what extent the bank will be willing to accommodate a delinquent debtor very often depends on the attitude and degree of cooperation of the debtor. Hard-pressed debtors often fail to understand the importance of establishing a cooperative, rather than an adversarial, relationship with the lender. At the first sign of trouble, the borrower should take the initiative to notify the bank and explain what is being done to remedy the situation. Expecting a bank to be sympathetic to one's plight and to make concessions seems unreasonable in cases where the borrower waits until the debt is long past due before approaching the lender to explain the problems. Additionally, a bank is not likely to be too sympathetic toward a borrower who fails to return phone calls and virtually disappears, or who is always "unavailable" to discuss the problem with the bank.

The lender is likely to be most cooperative with the hard-pressed debtor who alerts the bank to problems early on. The debtor should explain what efforts are being made to remedy the problems and keep in close contact with the bank, informing it of current developments and the progress made toward solution of the problems.

A favorably impressed lender can be an invaluable asset to your business not only in granting loans but also in helping you out in difficult times. Do not underestimate the need for establishing a solid, professional relationship with your lender. The ultimate success and growth of your business may well depend on it.

5

Selling Securities or Going Public

Whenever an individual or business sells a passive interest in the business, a security is involved. Securities include stocks, bonds, limited partnership interests, and certificates of participation in limited liability companies. There is some question as to whether a general partner's interest in a general partnership would be considered a security, though the law appears to favor a reality test. In fact, any so-called investment contract has been deemed to be a security. Whenever one party pledges cash or its equivalent in property in exchange for an interest in a project, a security is involved.

Exotic transactions, such as the purchase of profits from the ultimate sale of aged whiskey or profits from the sale of oranges growing on trees in an orange grove, have been declared to involve securities. The law in this regard is complex, and it is essential for you to work with an experienced business lawyer when attempting to obtain investments in your business.

Every sale of a security requires the seller or issuer to

comply with a host of legal formalities unless an exemption from compliance is available. The law governing securities is one of the most technical, and only experienced securities attorneys are generally in a position to counsel you about the requirements of a particular transaction. Even during the creation of a business entity, the securities law should be considered. Your attorney should determine whether an appropriate exemption from securities compliance is available or whether you must undertake the time-consuming and expensive process of registering the securities you will be issuing. Most small businesses are exempt from securities compliance, and their formative years will likely not involve a securities registration.

At some point you may determine that you wish to obtain capital from investors rather than borrow from lenders, and you may, therefore, consider having your business conduct a public securities offering. Each year hundreds of private businesses go public. In the first eight months of 1990 (the latest period for which figures are available), 191 companies raised approximately $8.69 billion through their initial public offerings. However, some small companies have become disillusioned with the supposed benefits of going public and are returning to their former private status. It is worthwhile to look at the pros and cons of going public and some of the factors you should consider before making that crucial decision.

Advantages of Going Public

Access to capital and increased prestige are the motivating forces behind going public. Issuing stock has the advantage of raising much-needed capital without draining the resources needed for daily operations. The additional capital allows for continued growth even when earnings and bank loans are insufficient to meet expansion objectives. Also, a successful public offering can improve net worth and debt-to-equity ratio, thereby increasing credibility and financing leverage with lenders.

Public offerings also enhance a company's prestige by increasing its visibility within the business community. The prestige of issuing stock is an effective device for attracting top-rate management executives. In turn, a strong management team is often the key to both increasing profitability and attracting new investors.

Disadvantages of Going Public

Disadvantages of going public are primarily high costs and diminished control over the company. The cost of going public includes extensive fees for printing, attorneys, accountants, filing fees, and underwriter commissions. Businesses contemplating a public offering should expect an initial outlay of $50,000 to $150,000. In addition, going public increases a business's administrative costs. Going public means more regulations to adhere to and more paperwork to process. Public corporations undergo extensive auditing and must gather and disseminate information for their shareholders. These additional administrative functions add to the overall cost of doing business.

While shareholders supply much-needed capital to a growing business, they also usurp a degree of control over the company's operations. Suddenly, management is beholden to a large number of investors whose interest in short-term profits may conflict with what is best for the long-term health of the business. Shareholders and the general public (including competitors) must also be apprised of otherwise private information, such as details about management, organization, executives, products, sales, and profit figures. Public divulgence of this information can put a business at a competitive disadvantage. Furthermore, minority shareholders have certain dissenter and minority rights that give them a voice disproportionate to the size of their holdings. These disadvantages—high costs and diminished control over the business—must be carefully weighed before undertaking the rigors of going public.

The Initial Public Offering

Deciding to go public and implementing that decision is a time-consuming and complicated task. A company must first determine whether it is in an appropriate position to make a public offering and then choose the optimal timing. Factors to consider include the availability of other means of financing, the degree of financial need, and the market conditions for the specific product or services being offered. Since an initial public offering (IPO) is highly complex, any business proceeding with an IPO needs to assemble a professional team to assist with the myriad legal and financial considerations that invariably arise. This support team should include experienced legal counsel, independent accountants, investment bankers, underwriters, and selling agents.

Federal and State Securities Laws

The complex nature of securities law underscores the need for experienced legal counsel. The laws are promulgated under both state and federal statutes. The Securities and Exchange Commission (SEC) is responsible for administering the federal securities laws. Its purpose is to assure equal access to and full disclosure of all material facts about a business. However, the SEC recognizes that the burden of disclosure is often excessive and nonessential as applied to smaller businesses. Consequently, special procedures and exemptions have been established for small businesses to simplify and expedite the registration process.

Compliance with federal law does not end the matter. A securities issuer must also comply with state provisions known as "blue sky" laws, which are sometimes even more stringent than the federal statutes. Consequently, stricter state provisions regarding the registration of small issues may offset the benefits of simplified procedures and exemptions under federal law. Nevertheless, the small business must comply with the stricter state provisions.

Violations of securities laws can result in civil or, in some cases, criminal liability. Sanctions include rescission of the entire offering, money damages, injunction against or voiding of business transactions, and even criminal prosecution. Furthermore, all securities, whether registered or exempt, are subject to strict antifraud provisions. Liability of the issuer is unlimited and extends to significant shareholders as well as to other related persons or entities.

The Attorney's Role

The particularly involved nature of securities law makes the experienced attorney an indispensable part of any successful public offering. The attorney must ensure adherence to all relevant laws and regulations. Attorneys must also make the company aware of possible exemptions, advise on necessary disclosures, and assist in preparing the necessary disclosure documents such as a prospectus and a registration statement. Furthermore, an experienced attorney can review existing contracts and advise changes, file necessary documents for SEC review, and recommend internal structural changes that will ease the company's transition from private to public.

The Accountant's Role

A significant part of any public offering is the accounting required by the SEC. Accountants must provide audits on the company to be sure that its financial data is current and, when appropriate, prepare earnings projections or forecasts. The accountant will work closely with the attorney during the registration process.

The Banker's Role

Many companies will need some interim or bridge financing before the offering is completed. The banker may assist with this interim financing. In addition, many companies are funded by a combination of financing vehicles such as conventional loans, lines of credit secured by inventory or accounts receivable or both, and traditional equity financing (stock). The banker will assist the company in determining its optimum funding mix. The banker will also aid the company in obtaining loans when appropriate.

The Underwriter's and Selling Agent's Roles

Rarely will a company be in a position to sell its own securities. It is, therefore, important for an underwriter to be retained for the purpose of placing the investment. Underwriters generally have a network of sales agents who will assist them in selling the company's securities. Generally, there are three kinds of underwriting:

1. In *firm underwriting,* the underwriter purchases the entire offering at a discount and resells it to investors. This is customarily used for very large, established companies with an existing public market.

2. In *standby underwriting,* the underwriter commits to sell a certain

amount of the offering and agrees to purchase up to that portion if it is not sold to investors. Again, this form of underwriting is customarily confined to large established companies with an existing public market in their securities.

3. *Best efforts* underwriting is the most common for IPOs, smaller companies, and private placements. In this form of underwriting, the underwriter merely agrees to use best efforts to sell the offering. There is no assurance, however, that the securities will actually be sold, nor any obligation on the underwriter to purchase unsold securities.

While many companies go public in order to satisfy business and other needs, some publicly traded companies have "gone private." The process of "privatizing" a public company is complex, but typically involves a situation whereby an individual company or group offers to purchase the stock or ownership interest from public holders for a price that exceeds the then-trading price of that security. This type of transaction is more likely when it is believed that the publicly traded company's potential value could be enhanced if the individual or group acquiring these securities had more control.

The process of taking a business private is as technical and demanding as the process of taking it public. Complying with the laws surrounding so-called tender offers and the rules imposed by the SEC necessitate the skills of experienced securities lawyers, investment bankers, underwriters, and the like.

Conclusion

The law surrounding securities is pervasive. It touches every transaction in which businesses obtain investments. Determining whether your business must comply with some or all of the federal and state securities laws is essential. You should work with your attorney, accountant, and business advisor in order to make this determination and avoid the undesirable consequences that may result from violating the securities laws.

6

Contracts

Contracts are an essential part of virtually every business. Clearly I cannot cover the entire field of contract law here, but perhaps I can help you become aware of some of the ramifications of contract law and enable you to see where you need to be cautious.

What Is a Contract?

A contract is a legally binding promise or set of promises. The law requires that the parties to a contract perform the promises they have made to each other. In the event of nonperformance—usually called a *breach*—the law provides remedies to the injured party. For the purposes of this discussion, we will assume that the contract is between two people, though it can involve business organizations as well.

The three basic elements of every contract are the *offer*, the *acceptance*, and the *consideration*. Suppose a salesperson shows a customer a Mustang convertible at an automobile lot and suggests that she buy it (the offer). The customer says she likes it and wants it (the acceptance). They agree on a price (the consideration). That is the basic framework, but a great many variations can be played on that theme.

Types of Contracts

Contracts may be *express* or *implied*; they may be *oral* or *written*. On this latter point, there are generally at least two types of contracts that *must* be in writing if they are to be legally enforceable:

- Any contract that by its terms cannot be completed in less than one year
- Any contract that involves the sale of goods for over $500

An express contract is one in which all the details are spelled out and can be either oral or written. Although, if you are going to the trouble of expressing contractual terms, you should put your understanding in writing. For example, you might make a contract with a retail store for six dozen gallons of apple cider to be delivered by you on October 1, at a price of $1.75 per gallon to be paid within thirty days of receipt. This scenario is fairly straightforward. If either party fails to live up to any material part of the contract, a breach has occurred, and the other party may withhold performance of his or her obligation until receiving assurance that the breaching party will perform. In the event no such assurance is forthcoming, the aggrieved party may have a cause of action and sue for breach of contract.

If the apple cider is delivered on October 15, and the store had advertised the availability of your special apple cider during the week of October 1, time was an important consideration, and the store would not be required to accept the late shipment. If time is not a material consideration, however, then even with the slight delay, this probably would be considered "substantial performance," and the store would have to accept the delivery.

Implied contracts are not usually not done in writing and need not be very complicated. An example might be if you call a supplier to order five boxes of computer paper without making any express statement that you will pay for the paper. The promise to pay is implied in the order and is enforceable when the paper is delivered.

But with implied contracts, things can often become a lot stickier. Suppose a manufacturer of notepads asks you to send over a supply of a new kind of glue you have just begun marketing to try it out. You deliver a generous amount. The notepad manufacturer likes the glue, uses it up, and is overheard commenting that it is the best glue yet for the manufacture of notepads. Is there an implied contract to purchase in this arrangement? That depends on whether you are normally in the business of giving away large free samples of new products.

You enter into many contracts without thinking much about them, such as those exchanges of promises that take place between your business and the company supplying your telephone service. (The telephone company agrees to provide certain telecommunications services in exchange for your promise to pay for those services under certain agreed-upon terms.) Perhaps the more problematic contracts are those that you enter into on a regular but intermittent basis for the purchase or sale of goods and services critical to the ongoing viability and smooth running of your business.

In order to examine the principles of offer, acceptance, and consideration, we will examine them in the context of several potential situations for hypothetical business owner Pat Smith. Smith is an automobile dealer who has an impressive collection of vintage cars restored to mint condition. Let us look at the following situations and see whether an enforceable contract comes into existence:

- At a cocktail party, Jones expresses an interest in Smith's cars. "It looks like the market value of your cars keeps going up," Jones tells Smith. "I'm going to buy one while I can still afford it."

Is this a contract? If so, what are the terms of the offer—the particular car, the specific price? No, this is not really an offer that Smith can accept. It is nothing more than an opinion or a vague expression of intent.

- Brown offers to pay $4,000 for one of Smith's cars that she saw in an auto show several weeks ago. At the show, it was listed at $4,500, but Smith agrees to accept the lower price.

Is this an enforceable contract? Yes! Brown has offered in unambiguous terms to pay a specific amount for a specific car, and Smith has accepted the offer. A binding contract exists.

- One day Jones shows up at Smith's vintage-auto lot and sees a particular car for which he offers $4,500. Smith accepts and promises to transfer title the next week, at which time Jones will pay for it. An hour later Brown shows up. She likes the same car and offers Smith $6,000 for it. Can Smith accept the later offer?

No—a contract exists with Jones. An offer was made and accepted. The fact that the object has not yet been delivered or paid for does not make the contract any less binding.

- Green discusses certain renovations he would like Smith to perform on a particular car Smith has just acquired. He offers to pay $6,000 for the car if the final product is satisfactory to him. Green approves preliminary sketches, and Smith completes the work. But when Green arrives to pick up his car, he refuses to accept it because it does not satisfy him.

Green is making the offer in this case, but the offer is conditional upon his satisfaction with the completed work. Smith can only accept the offer by producing something that meets Green's subjective standards—a risky business. There is no enforceable contract for payment until such time as Green indicates that the completed work is satisfactory.

Suppose Green comes to Smith's vintage car lot and says that the car is satisfactory but then when Smith delivers it, says he has changed his mind. That is too late. The contract became binding at the moment he indicated the work to be satisfactory. If he then refuses to accept it, he would be breaching his contract.

Earlier I mentioned that contracts for goods over $500 must be in writing. The last example described was of a hybrid sale, for goods and services. Since the goods involved were over $500 in value, the contract should be in writing to ensure enforceability. However, if the contract had been one for performance of personal services only—say, for renovation to be performed by Smith on Green's own car—the *Uniform Commercial Code* (UCC) would not apply, and the contract would be enforceable whether it was reduced to writing or not. (The UCC is a compilation of commercial laws enacted in some form in every state, though Louisiana has not adopted the sections discussed in this chapter.)

Oral or Written Contracts?

Contracts are enforceable only if they can be proven. All the hypothetical examples mentioned above could have been oral contracts, but a great deal of detail is often lost in the course of remembering a conversation. The best practice, of course, is to get it in writing. The function of a written contract is not only that of proof, but to make very clear the understanding of the parties regarding the agreement and the terms of the contract.

Some smaller business owners prefer to do business strictly on the basis of a handshake, particularly with their immediate suppliers and retailers. The assumption seems to be that the best business relations are those based upon mutual trust alone. Although there may be some validity to this, business owners nevertheless really should put all oral agreements into writing. Far too many trusting people have suffered adverse consequences because of their idealistic reliance upon the sanctity of oral contracts.

Under even the best of business relationships it is still possible that one or both parties might forget the terms of an oral agreement. It is also possible that both parties might have quite different perceptions about the precise terms of the agreement reached. When the agreement is put into writing, however, there is much less doubt as to the terms of the arrangement. Thus, a written contract generally functions as a safeguard against subsequent misunderstanding or forgetful minds.

Perhaps the principal problem with oral contracts lies in the fact that they cannot always be proven or enforced. Proof of oral contracts typically centers around the conflicting testimony of the parties involved. If one of the parties is not able to establish by a preponderance of evidence that his or her version of the contract is the correct one, then the oral contract may be considered nonexistent—as though it had never been made. The same result might occur if the parties cannot remember the precise terms of the agreement, and memories do fade.

When Written Contracts Are Necessary

Even if an oral contract is established, it may not always be enforceable. As already noted, there are some agreements that must be in writing in order to be legally enforceable.

An early law that was designed to prevent fraud and perjury, known as the Statute of Frauds, provides that any contract, which by its terms cannot be fully performed within one year, must be in writing. This rule is narrowly interpreted, so if there is *any* possibility no matter how remote that the contract *could* be fully performed within one year, the contract need not be reduced to writing.

For example, if a jeweler agreed to submit one piece of custom-designed jewelry to a customer each year for a period of five years, the contract would have to be in writing. By the very terms of the agreement there is no way the contract could be performed within one year. If, on the other hand, the contract called for the jeweler to deliver five pieces within a period of five years, the contract would not have to be in writing under the Statute of Frauds. It is possible, though perhaps not probable, that the jeweler could deliver all five pieces within the first year. The fact that the jeweler does not actually complete performance of the contract within one year is immaterial. So long as complete performance within one year is within the realm of possibility, the contract need not be in writing to be enforceable; it may be oral.

The Statute of Frauds further provides that any contract for the sale of goods valued at $500 or more is not enforceable unless it has been put into writing and signed by the party against whom enforcement is being sought. The fact that a contract for a price in excess of $500 is not in writing does not void the agreement or render it illegal. The parties are free to perform the oral arrangement, but if one party refuses to perform, the other will be unable to legally enforce the agreement.

The law defines *goods* as all things that are movable at the time the contract is made, except for the money used as payment. The real question becomes whether a particular contract involves the sale of goods for a price of $500 or more. Although the answer would generally seem to be fairly clear, ambiguities may arise.

For example, if a supplier agrees to provide a business with all its stationery needs for the coming year, how is the price to be determined? If the jeweler sells a number of pieces to a customer where the total purchase price exceeds $500, but the price of the individual works is less than $500, which price governs? In light of these possible ambiguities, the safest course is to put all oral contracts into writing. Most states have additional circumstances requiring contracts to be in writing, so you should contact your attorney before entering into any important oral contract.

No-Cost Written Agreements

At this point, owners of small businesses might object, asserting that they do not have the time, energy, or patience to draft contracts. After all, they are in business to make a product or sell a service, not to formulate written contracts steeped in legal jargon.

Fortunately, the businessperson will not always be required to do this since the supplier or retailer may be willing to draft a satisfactory contract. However, be wary of signing any form contracts—*they will almost invariably be one-sided*, with all terms in favor of whoever paid to have them drafted.

As a second alternative, the businessperson could employ an attorney to draft contracts, but this might be worthwhile only for substantial transactions. With respect to smaller transactions, the legal fees may be much larger than the benefits derived from having a written contract.

The Uniform Commercial Code provides businesses with a third and perhaps the best alternative. Remember, however, that the UCC applies only to the sale of goods. In situations where the UCC applies, businesses need not draft contracts or rely on anyone else (a supplier, retailer, or attorney) to do so.

The UCC provides that where both parties are merchants and one party sends to the other a written confirmation of an oral contract, within a reasonable time after that contract was made, and the recipient does not object to the confirming memorandum within ten days of its receipt, the contract will be deemed enforceable.

A *merchant* is defined as any person who normally deals in goods of the kind sold or who, because of occupation, represents him- or herself as having knowledge or skill peculiar to the practices or goods involved in the transaction. Most businesspeople will be considered merchants.

It should be emphasized that the sole effect of the confirming memorandum is that neither party can use the Statute of Frauds as a defense, assuming that the recipient fails to object within ten days after receipt. The party sending the confirming memorandum must still prove that an oral contract was made prior to or at the same time as the written confirmation. However, once such proof is offered, neither party can raise the Statute of Frauds to avoid enforcement of the agreement.

The advantage of the confirming memorandum over a written contract lies in the fact that the confirming memorandum can be used without the active participation of the other contracting party. It would suffice, for example, to simply state: "This memorandum is to confirm our oral agreement."

Since you would then still have to prove the terms of that agreement, it would be useful to provide a bit more detail in the confirming memorandum such as the subject of the contract, the date it was made, and the price or other consideration to be paid. Thus, you might draft something like the following:

> This memorandum is to confirm our oral agreement made on July 3, 1991, pursuant to which supplier agreed to deliver to purchaser on or before September 19, 1991, five thousand sheets of letterhead for the purchase price of $600.

The advantages of providing some detail in the confirming memorandum are twofold. First, in the event of a dispute, you could introduce the memorandum as proof of the terms of the oral agreement. Second, the recipient of the memorandum will be precluded from offering any proof regarding the terms of the oral contract that contradicts the terms contained in the memorandum. The recipient, or for that matter the party sending the memorandum, can introduce proof only regarding the terms of the oral contract that are consistent with the terms, if any, found in the memorandum. Thus, the purchaser in the above example would be precluded from claiming that the contract called for delivery of ten thousand sheets of letterhead because the quantity was stated in the written memo and not objected to. On the other hand, the purchaser would be permitted to testify that the oral contract required the supplier to engrave the letterhead in a specific way since this testimony would not be inconsistent with the terms stated in the memorandum.

One party to a contract can prevent the other from adding or inventing terms that are not spelled out in the confirming memorandum by ending the memorandum with a clause requiring all other provisions to be contained in a written and signed document. Such a clause might read:

> This is the entire agreement between the parties and no modification, alteration, or additional terms shall be enforceable unless in writing and signed by both parties.

If you use such a clause, be sure there are no additional agreed-to terms that have not been included in the written document. A court will generally be confined to the four corners of the document when trying to determine what was agreed to between the parties. An exception to this rule is that a court may allow oral evidence for the purpose of interpreting ambiguities or explaining the meaning of certain technical terms. The parties may also permit the other parties to introduce evidence of past practices in connection with the contract in question, in connection with other agreements between the parties, or even in connection with contracts between other parties.

To sum up, businesspeople should not rely on oral contracts alone since they offer little protection in the event of a dispute. The best protection is afforded by a written contract. It is a truism that oral contracts are not worth the paper they are written on. If drafting a complete written contract proves too burdensome or too costly, the businessperson should at least submit a memorandum in confirmation of the oral contract. That at least surpasses the initial barrier raised by the Statute of Frauds. Moreover, by recounting the terms in the memorandum, the businessperson is in a much better position to prove the oral contract at a later date.

Essentials to Put in Writing

A written contract rarely need be—or should be—a long, complicated document written in legal jargon designed to provide a handsome income to lawyers. A contract should be written in simple language that both parties can understand and should spell out the terms of the agreement.

A contract should include the following:

- The date of the agreement
- Identification of the two parties, e.g., the buyer and seller in the case of sale of goods or services
- A description of the goods or services sold
- The price or other consideration
- The signatures of the parties involved

To supplement these basics, an agreement should spell out whatever other terms might be applicable, such as pricing arrangements, payment schedules, insurance coverage, and consignment details. Many transactions are important enough that additional clauses covering certain contingencies should be added as well.

Finally, it should be noted that a written document that leaves out essential terms of the contract presents many of the same problems of proof and ambiguity as an oral contract. The terms of the contract should be well conceived, clearly drafted, "conspicuous" (i.e., not in tiny print that no one can read), and in "plain English" so everyone can understand them.

7

Consignment

There are many commercial arrangements by which merchandise may be sold. The most common are either outright purchase or *consignment*. In the outright purchase arrangement, merchandise is acquired, title is transferred from the seller to the buyer, and the purchase price is due when the goods are delivered. On the other hand, under a typical consignment arrangement, the consignor delivers an item to a dealer or consignee. The consignee does not make an outright purchase of the goods, but rather agrees to remit to the consignor the proceeds of sales less the consignment commission as the sales are made. Generally, the consignee is under no obligation to sell the goods and may return them to the consignor at any time.

Advantages and Disadvantages of Consignment

Although it may not be immediately obvious, the consignment arrangement can be beneficial to both parties. For the consignee, consignments eliminate much of the financial risk of carrying goods of questionable market appeal. If the item does not sell or sells poorly, the consignee will generally not lose much money since it has made no direct investment by purchasing the piece. The consignee loses only to the extent that the display space filled by the consigned work could have been filled by other items having greater sales potential along with whatever amount of money was expended on advertising, overhead, etc.

The advantage to the consignor is that consignment provides an opportunity to get a product into retail outlets where it might not otherwise be accepted. Another advantage is that the consignor generally gets a larger share of the retail selling price—around 60 percent in consignment versus 50 percent in wholesaling. (That is changing, however, and consignment percentages are getting closer and closer to the 50 percent wholesale arrangement.)

Conversely, there are several deterrents to consignment, which often make people reluctant to engage in consignment selling. After all, it is the consignor who takes most of the risks in such arrangements, and a number of questions are bound to arise: How promptly does the consignee pay after the work is sold? Is the work insured while it is on the consignee's premises? Will unsold work be returned in good condition? In addition, there is all the paperwork and recordkeeping.

Other deterrents to the consignment arrangement are more complicated. What happens, for example, if a consignor delivers work to a consignee and the consignee then goes bankrupt? What if the goods are destroyed by fire or stolen while on the consignee's premises? What if the consignee fails to pay debts to a creditor who has a security interest in all the consignee's assets including the consigned work? The resolution of these questions depends upon a determination of which party, the consignor on the one hand or the creditor or bankruptcy trustee on the other, has priority over the consigned work. There is no question that all these parties may have valid claims to the work; the question is rather which claim is to be given first priority.

If a Consignee Goes Bankrupt

Before the enactment of the Uniform Commercial Code (UCC), the consignor would generally prevail over the consignee's creditors or the consignee's trustee in bankruptcy with respect to the consigned item. Moreover, the consignor would prevail even though there was no record of the consignment that would give creditors or a trustee in bankruptcy notice of the consignment's existence. In effect, the consignor held a secret lien on the consigned work that was given priority over all other liens.

However the UCC revised the rule of priority largely in response to the general consensus that secret liens should not be legally enforceable. Thus, Article 2 of the UCC provides that where a consignor delivers work to a business dealing in goods of the kind consigned, the consignor will not have priority over the claims of creditors or a trustee in bankruptcy unless the consignor meets at least one of the following conditions:

1. Complies with the applicable state law providing that the consignor's interest be indicated by a sign on the goods
2. Establishes in court that the consignee is known by its creditors to be substantially engaged in selling goods under consignment
3. Complies with the filing requirements in Article 9 of the UCC

As to the first option, most states do not have sign laws. Even in those states that do, the consignor should not rely on the consignee to place and maintain a sign on the goods indicating that they have been consigned since it may not be in the interests of the consignee to do so. For example, a retailer would generally be in a much better position to obtain loans if a lending institution was led to believe that all the work in the store was owned outright as opposed to being consigned.

Moreover, the consignor should not expect to prevail under the second option since it will generally be difficult to prove that the consignee was known by the creditors to be substantially engaged in the business of selling consigned goods.

This leaves the third option. As a general rule, the consignor can best protect a consigned item by complying with the filing provisions contained in Article 9 of the UCC.

The purpose of the Article 9 filing requirement is simply to give notice to interested parties that certain property is subject to outstanding interests. The filing requirement gives notice to creditors, lending institutions, and the like that the item in the retail outlet is subject to a consignment agreement between the retailer and the consignor.

That process requires the filing of financial statements with the secretary of state in every state where the consigned goods are located, paying filing fees each time, giving notice to the consignee's creditors, and several other requirements.

There has been considerable debate as to whether the UCC provisions adequately safeguard the consignor's interests under consignment arrangements. As an initial consideration, there is the problem that the consignor may not even be aware that the protection exists. Many people who are just getting a business started are unaware of certain details of business and law such as consignor protection.

Moreover, even the consignor who knows that the potential for protection exists may be unable or unwilling to learn how that protection may be secured. In the case of complying with the filing requirements of Article 9, many who know what is required may find that approach too complex and bothersome.

Special Laws for Artists

As a result of these problems and others, several states have enacted special artist-dealer consignment laws. The first of these laws was enacted by the state of New York in 1966. Thereafter, California, Colorado, Connecticut, District of Columbia, Florida, Idaho, Illinois, Iowa, Kentucky, Maryland, Massachusetts, Michigan, Minnesota, Missouri, Montana, New Hampshire, New Jersey, New Mexico, New York, North Carolina, Ohio, Oregon, Pennsylvania, Tennessee, Texas, Washington, and Wisconsin passed similar legislation. Other states are considering such laws largely in response to increasing pressures from artists and arts organizations.

Although each state has enacted its own unique version, the basic provisions of artist-dealer consignment laws are essentially the same. Most statutes provide that any works of art delivered to any art dealer are presumed to be delivered under a consignment arrangement unless the artist has been paid in full on or before delivery. Thus, the majority of transactions between artists and various art dealers will be deemed consignments for purposes of these statutes.

In addition, most artist-dealer consignment statutes provide that all consigned artwork, as well as the proceeds from sale of the artwork, will be held in trust by the art dealer on behalf of the artist. This basically means that the art dealer will be solely responsible for any loss, theft, or damage occurring to the consigned artwork or the proceeds from the sales thereof that could have been avoided had the art dealer exercised the utmost care and caution. A few statutes go further by imposing *absolute liability* upon the art dealer for loss or damage, i.e., the art dealer will be liable for loss or damage to the consigned artwork even though such loss or damage could not have been avoided by the utmost care and caution.

Several of the laws require the artist and dealer to enter into a written agreement containing at least the following information: the value of the artwork, the minimum price for which it can be sold, and the percentage to be paid to the dealer. Of course the contract can contain more provisions, though an attempt to avoid the protective provisions of the consignment legislation is generally prohibited by the laws.

Finally, and perhaps most importantly, nearly all these statutes provide that the consigned artwork is protected against all claims made by the art dealer's creditors including the trustee in bankruptcy. Thus, at least one effect of the consignment legislation is to provide artists with protection similar to that afforded by Article 9 of the UCC without requiring the artist to take any steps to procure that protection.

Artwork: Covered or Not?

Although art-consignment legislation would seem to solve many of the practical problems with consignments of art, artists should review how the applicable legislation, if any, defines the terms *art dealer* and *artwork*. Fortunately, an art dealer has been broadly defined by nearly all states as being any person engaged in the business of selling artwork other than a person exclusively engaged in the business of selling goods at public auction. On the other hand, artwork has sometimes been given a rather narrow definition. Some statutes have defined artwork as including only the traditional areas of fine art such as painting, sculpture, and drawing. This means that under some consignment statutes the product of the craftsperson may not be deemed to be within the purview of the statutory protection.

Other statutes expressly include such items as those made of clay, fiber, wood, metal, plastic, or glass as being within the definition of a work of art protected by the legislation.

Conclusion

Consignment arrangements can provide manufacturers and distributors with expanded sales potential; yet it is necessary to determine whether some protection may be available for the consigned goods. Fine artists in many states have been granted automatic protection for their consigned works. Unfortunately for other businesspeople, these laws are not all-encompassing. It is therefore prudent to determine what protection is available for your business when engaging in a consignment transaction and to evaluate the costs versus benefits available from complying with the applicable laws.

8

Collections

There are several ways to deal with collection problems, ranging from preventive action to initiating a lawsuit. If you are fortunate enough to deal with people who always pay their bills on time, the remaining portion of this chapter may be of no interest at all. If, however, you have experienced delays in payment or have had some totally uncollectible bills, you should consider the suggestions that follow.

The general rule in a sales transaction is that payment is due upon delivery of the item being sold. While this rule may be subject to technical complications that are beyond the scope of this discussion, it basically means that upon delivery of merchandise to a customer, or completion of a project for the customer, the seller has the legal right to demand payment in full at that moment. This assumes that no arrangement has been made between the buyer and the seller allowing the purchaser to delay payment.

While payment upon delivery is common in retail transactions, it is unusual when selling on consignment or in transactions between manufacturers and distributors. In addition, the purchase of a rather expensive item may be subject to an installment-payment arrangement.

Point-of-Sale Payments

Manufacturers who deal directly with the public at shows, fairs, or their own shops customarily expect to be paid at the moment they make the sale, before the item is taken away by the customer. Such payment is made by currency, check, or credit card. Therefore, it is necessary for you to determine whether the currency is authentic, whether the credit card will be honored, and whether the check is going to be honored by the bank. Obviously, the cash sale is the safest way, though you should be aware that counterfeiting is not a thing of the past.

Currency

Identifying counterfeit currency is usually very technical and difficult. Occasionally, however, it is simple if the counterfeiter has made a glaring error such as using George Washington on a five-dollar bill. The federal government is quite diligent in alerting business people to the presence of counterfeit currency in a particular area when it is aware of the problem. The best way to avoid being stuck with a counterfeit bill is to keep your eyes open. It is a good idea not to accept any bill larger than $50.

Credit Cards

With regard to credit card fraud, the first thing to do is to compare the signature on the back of the card with the signature on the credit card slip. Even more important is to follow the credit card company's procedures carefully. If the company requires you to get authorization for all credit card sales over $50, then be sure to get that authorization. It may seem time-consuming and troublesome, but the rules are based on bitter experience. If you have made a credit card sale without following the instructions, and the credit card turns out to have been stolen or the buyer has exceeded his or her credit limit, you are likely to be stuck with the loss.

Personal Checks

The most frequent problems occur over personal checks. A host of things can prevent a check from being honored or cashed by a bank. To begin with, the person who writes the check may be an impostor using a checkbook that actually belongs to someone else. In order to reduce the likelihood of this occurrence, you should insist upon seeing at least two pieces of identification, one of which should, ideally, contain a photograph of the person. A current credit card, or a check guarantee card with photo and signature facsimile are also good. Do not accept as identification such items as Social Security cards, library cards, or any ID that can be easily obtained or forged.

Watch while the person signs the check (signatures may have been previously traced from a valid signature) and compare the signature with that of the other identification. While only an expert can identify a good forgery, most people can recognize a clumsy attempt by an amateur.

Accept checks only if they are made out to you, and only if they are written for the exact amount of the sale. In other words, do not take checks made out to someone else and endorsed to you, never *cash* a check, and do not take checks for more than the sale amount—that is, when you have to give change in cash.

Assuming that the individual writing the check is legitimate, there are still more potential problems. One of the most common difficulties is the problem of insufficient funds to cover the check. If the amount of your sale is substantial, it is prudent to request a certified or bank-guaranteed check. However, the inconvenience of requiring the purchaser to have a check certified may interfere with impulse sales, and is thus not practical for many retailers.

If the person writing the check is known to you, it is less likely the person will give you a bad check. Even if the buyer is a stranger, the risk of receiving a bad check and not being able to locate the buyer afterward can be reduced if the buyer's address and phone number are copied onto the check from the supporting pieces of identification if they are different from those printed on the face of the check.

Despite all these precautions, some bad checks do slip through. It is a crime in most states to pay for something with a check that the signer knows will be dishonored. A lawsuit can be brought against a buyer to recover the amount of the check. If you win such a suit, most states will allow the recovery of reasonable costs of litigation including the attorney's fees.

A check returned for insufficient funds can be redeposited in the hope that the check will be covered the second time through. Some bad checks are simply the result of a miscalculation of account balance or of the buyer having received a bad check. It is always a good idea to make a phone call before filing a lawsuit!

Consignment

If you sell manufactured goods through a retailer, at least two payment arrangements are possible. First, the goods may be consigned, and payment is due only after the actual sale of the item. Unfortunately, it is not uncommon for a retailer to neglect to inform a manufacturer of sales or to delay notification for an unreasonably long period of time. Furthermore, when retail outlets are forced into bankruptcy, you can lose your consigned goods. As was discussed in chapter 7, a consignor is well advised to take steps to protect consigned goods from the consignee's creditors. These measures are covered under the Uniform Commercial Code and are particularly important in states where specific consignment-protection legislation does not exist.

Invoicing

The other method of payment is after you have submitted an invoice to a wholesale buyer. Invoices are commonly paid within a specified time, usually thirty days after they have been tendered. This system virtually guarantees that you will not receive payment until the invoice is due. Indeed, unless some inducement for early payment is offered, you may wait interminably to be paid.

Ways of Encouraging Payment

Cash Discounts

By offering a cash discount, you can encourage early payment in a simple way. The offer of a 5 percent cash discount for early or even on-time payment may be all the encouragement some purchasers need. If the buyers earn more interest on their cash reserves than is offered as a discount, buyers will likely ignore the cash discount.

Charging Interest on Overdue Payments: Pros and Cons

The other option that can be combined with the incentive of cash discounts is to charge interest on payments received after the invoice due date. This method involves two possible traps. First, many states still have usury laws limiting the percent of interest that can be charged. A lender who exceeds the legal interest ceiling may find that the entire debt is forfeited, that all interest is forfeited, or that a usury penalty is imposed.

The second possible problem is the necessity to comply with the federal Truth-in-Lending Act and the various equivalent state laws. The Truth-in-Lending Act is basically a disclosure law that requires certain terms be included on any contract or billing that charges interest. The required disclosures have recently been simplified, and the task of compliance is further eased by the availability of preprinted forms containing the required disclosures. While many of the required terms may seem inapplicable to a simple sales transaction, you are well advised if you want to charge interest to use a form that contains all the disclosures. These forms are available from legal publishers and private attorneys.

When the Payment Never Comes

If neither the carrot nor the stick is effective in obtaining payment, you have several other options. The first possibility is to do nothing. If the amount is small enough, you may simply decide not to pursue collection. Needless to say, if this alternative is selected, you should refrain from doing any future business with that customer. A second option might be to hire a collection agency to attempt to collect the debt. Collection agencies generally charge a commission of 10 to 30 percent of the recovered amount, though some agencies require an upfront fee and take a lower percentage, and still others charge a fixed fee.

Lawsuit

A third option is the instigation of a full-scale lawsuit to force payment. In many states, a formal demand for payment must be made prior to commencing a lawsuit. Moreover, this option is practical only if the outstanding debt is relatively large since an attorney must be hired and will likely be quite expensive, particularly if the case proceeds all the way to trial.

The court fees charged for filing a case can be rather high, ranging from $40 in some states and courts to over $150 in others. The defendant(s) (the debtor) must be personally served with court papers, which costs an additional $15 to $20 or more per defendant depending on the difficulty of service. Lastly, if the case is won and the buyer still refuses to pay, further proceedings must be initiated at additional cost to "execute" or force payment on the judgment received. All in all, on a moderate debt the expense involved in a civil trial may amount to more than the debt itself.

Small Claims Court

A simpler and less expensive solution on small debts is to bring an action in small claims court. While the rules vary from state to state, all the systems are geared toward making the process as swift, accessible, and inexpensive as possible. Moreover, most courts have staff members who help guide people through pleading in small claims court.

The major cost savings in a small claims court proceeding results from the fact that attorneys are not customarily permitted in such courts. Unless they represent themselves or a corporation, attorneys generally may not prepare required documents or appear in court. Even in states where attorneys are not specifically barred by statute, the court rules are set up in such a clear, comprehensible way that an attorney is usually not needed.

A small claims action has other advantages over a conventional lawsuit. However, not all actions can be brought in small claims court. As the name implies, only claims for small amounts can be brought. For example, *small* is defined as $3,500 in Oregon. Moreover, only actions seeking monetary damages are appropriate in small claims court; other forms of relief such as injunction cannot be granted.

The small claims process is comparatively swift and inexpensive. Filing fees are generally under $50. In addition, in most courts the creditor is not responsible for informing the debtor that a suit has been brought. The clerk of the court customarily mails the notice to the defendant by certified or registered mail. A small fee is generally charged to cover mailing costs.

In many states, the hearing on a small claims action may be held on a weekend or in the evening. The hearing itself is kept simple. The technical rules of evidence and of legal procedure are not followed. The judge simply hears both sides of the case and allows any evidence or the testimony of any witnesses either party has to offer. Jury trials are never permitted in small claims court, although the defendant may be able to have the case moved to a conventional court by demanding a jury trial.

An action in small claims court has disadvantages, too. First, the judgment is often absolutely binding, which means neither party may appeal. Where appeal is allowed, as in New York State, the party wishing to challenge the judgment must show that a grave injustice has been done. This is not easy.

The other major disadvantage to a small claims action is that the judgment may be uncollectible. In many states, the usual methods of enforcing a judgment—garnishment of wages or liens against property— are unavailable to the holder of a judgment from small claims court. Some jurisdictions permit a small claims court judgment to be converted into a traditional judgment, but this often requires the help of an attorney to assist with the process. In other states, such as New York, enforcement action can be taken only if the debt involved is the result of a business transaction, and the debtor has three other small claims court judgments outstanding.

For the most part, care in selecting those with whom you do business will minimize the need to use legal means to collect payment for sales. However, if all other methods fail, small claims court is by far the least expensive and easiest way to obtain legal redress for a small outstanding debt. The drawbacks should be considered, however, before you decide to use it as a remedy.

Bankruptcies

Straight Bankruptcy

There are two general categories of business bankruptcies. The first, referred to as *straight bankruptcy* in Chapter 7 of the bankruptcy law, contemplates the prompt conversion of all the bankrupt's nonexempt property to cash and the payment of creditors to the extent possible. The Bankruptcy law establishes a pecking order of creditors, giving some creditors priority for payment. Such creditors would be the U.S. government for taxes, and secured parties for the amount of their security interests. Each category of creditor must be paid in full before a lower-priority creditor may be paid at all. If there is not sufficient money to satisfy all creditors in a particular class, the members of that group will receive a pro rata portion of their claim.

There are some things among the bankrupt's assets that may be retained, even after bankruptcy, such as a modest house, a holy book, clothing, and the like. The list of exempt property varies from state to state.

After the bankrupt's nonexempt assets are completely distributed, the court-appointed trustee will apply to the bankruptcy judge for a discharge order. If the bankrupt has fulfilled all requirements of the Bankruptcy law, and the judge is satisfied with the proceeding, then the bankrupt's debts will be wiped out—or *discharged*—and the proceeding will end. Certain claims, however, cannot be discharged in bankruptcy. For example, any creditor who was not notified of the bankruptcy and given a chance to participate in the proceeding will have a claim that remains viable even after the bankruptcy proceeding has ended.

Reorganization

The second type of bankruptcy proceeding is the so-called Chapter 11, or *reorganization*, contemplating a somewhat different process. Rather than terminating the business, a Chapter 11 is designed to facilitate an orderly payment to creditors so that the business may survive.

When the Chapter 11 petition is filed and the creditors meet, a reorganization plan is proposed. All legal proceedings for debt collection other than the bankruptcy proceeding are frozen, and the bankrupt is given an opportunity to satisfy the creditors in a timely fashion. Once a plan acceptable to all creditors is prepared, it is presented to the bankruptcy judge. If it is determined that the Chapter 11 reorganization plan is "fair and equitable," the judge will approve it and it will be implemented.

Creditors customarily receive more under Chapter 11 than they do under straight bankruptcy, although reorganization is feasible only for a healthy business suffering a temporary economic reversal. Creditors who have a secured position, such as those who have filed UCC documents to establish their security interests (discussed in chapter 7), participate in drafting the Chapter 11 plan. Generally, these creditors would be those who sold on consignment or those who retain a security interest for the purchase price of some goods. A plan will be deemed "fair and equitable" to the secured creditors, and they may be forced to agree to it if it provides that they do any of the following:

- Retain their liens and receive future cash payments equal to the value of the security
- Retain a lien on the proceeds from the sale of their collateral
- Receive the equivalent of their interests such as cash up front or substituted collateral

In a Chapter 11 proceeding, a secured creditor may be forced to accept a less favorable position than the UCC would allow in order to have the plan accepted by all the creditors. Even though this may happen on occasion, someone with a security interest is still far better off than one who is unsecured.

Individuals may file a so-called Chapter 13 bankruptcy. In this type of arrangement, a plan is worked out so that the individual may pay ordinary and necessary living expenses. Any amounts earned over and above the amounts required for daily existence will be paid to a trustee for ultimate distribution to creditors.

Common sense, diligence, and attention to detail are always important attributes for any businessperson. When the economy is weak and money is tight, they become essential. There will probably always be some deadbeats and some uncollectible bills. But with proper care and some preventive attention, you can keep these to a minimum.

9

Expanding Your Market

Most successful businesses begin with a novel idea that is nurtured and grows into a profitable enterprise. The entrepreneur invests time, money, and energy into developing the concept, perhaps manufacturing the product or marketing the service. The entrepreneur may have also worked on expanding the business when and where appropriate.

Franchising

An alternative for some businesses is the franchise. A franchise is a right, or license, to follow an established, successful pattern. It also allows the business to use the trademarks, recipes, advertising, and training provided through the "franchiser." Those who purchase franchise opportunities are more likely to succeed than those who start from scratch, since many of the mistakes that dissipate resources can be avoided. The purchaser of a franchise is literally acquiring the goodwill, know-how, and intellectual property of an established business.

Where do you begin looking? Perhaps the best source for a complete list of franchise opportunities offered today is the *Franchise Opportunity Handbook*, which is published by the U.S. Department of Commerce and can be obtained from that agency. This handbook lists most registered franchise opportunities in the United States and gives a brief description of the nature of the business, the amount of the franchise fee, and information about the franchiser-franchisee relationship.

The Federal Trade Commission (FTC) has adopted specific regulations for companies offering the sale of franchise opportunities. In addition, most states have adopted some sort of franchise regulation. For example, many states require franchise opportunities to be registered prior to sale. A typical franchise statute defines a franchise as an agreement by which:

1. A franchisee is granted the right to engage in the business of offering, selling, or distributing goods or services under a marketing plan or system formulated by a franchiser

2. The operation of the franchisee's business pursuant to such a plan or system is substantially associated with the franchiser's trademark, service mark, trade name, logo, advertising, or other commercial symbol designating a franchiser

3. The franchisee is required to give to the franchiser a payment or something of value (in legal terms, a valuable consideration) for the right to transact business in accordance with the marketing plan

All companies that offer franchise opportunities are required to file with the appropriate regulatory agencies. They must also prepare extensive disclosure statements for publication in the FTC's *Uniform Offering Circular.* By obtaining a copy of the *Uniform Offering Circular,* those interested in a franchise will find a wealth of material including the following:

1. Information identifying the franchiser, its affiliates, and the affiliates' business experience since joining the franchise

2. Information describing the business experience of each of the franchiser's officers, directors, and those management personnel

responsible for franchise services, training, and other aspects of the franchise program

3. A description of any lawsuits in which the franchiser and its officers, directors and management personnel have been involved

4. Information about any bankruptcies in which the franchiser and its officers, directors, and management personnel have been involved

5. Information about the initial franchise fee and other payments that are required to obtain the franchise

6. A description of the continuing payments franchisees are required to make after a franchise is acquired

7. Information about any restrictions on the quality of goods and services used in the franchise, where those goods and services can be purchased, and any restrictions requiring that purchases be made from the franchiser or its affiliates

8. A description of any assistance available from the franchiser or its affiliates in financing the purchase of the franchise

9. A list of restrictions on the goods or services franchisees are permitted to market

10. A description of any restrictions on the customers with whom franchisees may deal

11. A description of any territorial limitations affecting the franchisee

12. A list of the conditions under which the franchise may be re-purchased or refused renewal by the franchiser, transferred to a third party by the franchisee, or terminated or modified by either party

13. A description of the training programs available to franchisees

14. A statement regarding the involvement of any celebrities or public figures in the franchise

15. A description of any assistance the franchiser will provide in selecting a site for the franchise

16. Statistical information about the present number of franchises, the number of franchises projected for the future, the number of franchises terminated, the number the franchiser has decided not to renew, and the number repurchased in the past

17. The financial statements of the franchiser

18. A description of the extent to which franchisees must personally participate in the operation of a franchise
19. A complete statement of the basis for any earnings claims made to the franchisee, including the percentage of existing franchises that have actually achieved the results that are claimed
20. A list of the names and addresses of other franchisees

After reviewing the information in the offering circular, the potential franchisee should ask some hard questions about the opportunity. What sort of controls will the franchiser require of the franchisee with respect to sale of product, territory, etc.? What controls over advertising or promises regarding advertising does the franchiser make? Has the franchiser appropriately protected the trademark in the federal Trademark Office and at the state level? Is the franchise for an indefinite term or must it be renewed on a periodic basis? What are the terms of renewal? Does the franchiser's system seem to be workable, understandable, and able to provide benefits necessary to justify the expense of paying a franchise fee?

There is a cost involved in acquiring a franchise and you must determine whether you are willing to pay that cost to acquire a franchise rather than creating your own business identity. There are pros and cons to both approaches and it is important for you to consider the costs, benefits, risks, and rewards before undertaking either course.

One of the major sacrifices to be made when acquiring a franchise opportunity is that of creating your own business identity and perhaps franchising it to others. By acquiring a franchise, you are purchasing some degree of security in exchange for the potential that might be realized from your own creation. You should also be aware of some franchise abuses that have surfaced.

Many franchisees have been injured when the franchiser permits competition within a comparatively small geographic area or establishes a company owned and operated location in close proximity to an existing franchise operation. If the franchiser fails to honor its commitment, will a franchisee be in a position to redress these wrongs?

It is quite clear that the purchase of a franchise ranks as a significant investment. Before you make that investment you should check out the pertinent information exhaustively, including consulting your business attorney and accountant and contacting other franchisees to learn about their experiences with the franchiser.

Multilevel Marketing

Another method of doing business is known as *multilevel marketing* (MLM). The leading companies in this field have surpassed billion-dollar sales marks and their stocks are traded on the New York Stock Exchange. Amway, Mary Kay, and Shaklee are MLMs that have become household names. Many MLM companies advertise through infomercials. During the past few years, product lines have expanded dramatically. The corporations involved market everything from computers and video equipment to healthcare products, art, and long-distance telephone services.

Simply stated, multilevel marketing is a form of marketing in which distributors or sales representatives sell products directly to the consumer. In most cases, distributors purchase the company product at wholesale and profit from the difference between the wholesale and retail prices. In other cases, a distributor functions as a sales representative who takes orders for company products or services—for example, long-distance discount telephone services—and receives a commission for whatever is sold.

Distributors are entitled to sponsor other distributors or sales representatives and receive commissions on the sales of the sponsored reps as well as on the sales of any further representatives sponsored in a continuous "down line." For a successful distributor, the rewards can be substantial.

Any system that offers dramatic rewards and carries with it a low cost of entry will obviously tend to attract some of the best and some of the worst individuals. The system has not always thrived. Over the years it has come perilously close to extinction as a result of prosecution by regulators who claimed the method promoted "pyramid schemes" under the guise of legitimate marketing. In many cases, the prosecutors were rightly chasing and eradicating unlawful pyramids.

Other programs that were legitimate have survived. In a landmark legal decision in 1979, the Amway Corporation prevailed in such a prosecution and in fact received a stamp of approval for its marketing program by the

FTC. This particular decision opened the door to many other legitimate multilevel marketing companies.

Protective Regulations

Because of the abuses in the industry, multilevel marketing has become closely scrutinized. Regulations regarding multilevel marketing companies in the United States are a constantly changing patchwork of overlapping laws, which vary from state to state. The basic thrust of these statutes is to prohibit marketing plans that require sales representatives to invest in the company or purchase the right to recruit others for economic gain. The statutes are designed to ensure that multilevel marketing companies are bona fide retail organizations that must market bona fide products to the consumer. Inventory loading, such as requiring distributors to purchase a minimum amount of the product and head-hunting, or remuneration for the mere act of recruiting others, are prohibited. Sales or sample kits and other marketing materials must be sold to sales representatives at actual company cost or provided free of charge.

What to Look For

If you are considering working with an MLM company, you should be aware of the following types of abuses that have been targeted as potential elements of illegal marketing plans:
1. Products that have no "real world" marketplace
2. Products that are sold at inflated prices
3. Plans that result in inventory loading by distributors
4. Substantial cash investment requirements
5. Mandatory purchases of peripheral or accessory products or services
6. Plans in which distributors are left with substantial unsold inventory upon cancellation of participation
7. Plans in which fees are paid to distributors for headhunting and emphasis is on recruitment rather than the sale of product
8. Misrepresentations or inflated representations of earnings

In determining whether or not a program is a legitimate multilevel marketing opportunity, the would-be participant or the entrepreneur who is considering starting a multilevel marketing program should keep in mind several important points:

- *Product* The company should offer a high-quality product in which consumer satisfaction is guaranteed. It must have a demand in the marketplace. If the product is one consumed by distributors themselves, it must be one that distributors would want to buy on its own merits, irrespective of participation in the marketing plan.
- *Price* The price of the product must be fair and competitive. Distributors should be able to purchase the product at wholesale or at a substantial discount from prices found in retail stores.
- *Investment Requirement* There should be no investment requirement at all except for a sales or sample kit or demonstration materials sold at company cost or provided free.
- *Purchase and Inventory Requirements* A legitimate marketing program should have no minimum-purchase requirement nor any inventory requirement for someone to become or remain a qualified distributor or sales representative.
- *Sales Commission* Sales commissions should not be paid for the mere act of sponsoring other distributors.
- *Buyback Policy* A legitimate multilevel marketing company will agree to buy back inventory and sales materials in resellable condition from distributors who cancel participation in the program.
- *Retail Sales* The focus of the marketing program should be to promote retail sales to nonparticipants.
- *Distributor Activity* Many of the statutes regarding multilevel distribution companies require that distributors perform a bona fide, supervisory, distributive selling, or soliciting function in moving the product to the consumer.
- *Earnings Statements* The basic rule is that a legitimate marketing program should not make any earnings representations unless those statements are based on a verifiable track record of average earnings of distributors in a particular geographic area.

MLM is an established marketing process. Whether it is right for you is an important consideration. You must be willing to actively promote sales of the product while continuing to recruit individuals to augment your "down line." It is only through both activities that you are likely to earn significant returns. Before agreeing to become a distributor for an MLM company, you should be sold on the product itself and not merely the prospect of getting rich from the activities of others. MLM distributing is hard work! The time devoted to this activity can be considerable and may preclude you from developing other business opportunities.

There are numerous other business opportunities that may be available to an energetic entrepreneur. These include, among many others, the ability to acquire an existing business, buy into a partnership or other business, or invest in someone else's business dream. Many states have laws regulating the promotion, advertisement, and sale of business opportunities. Some of these laws are broad enough to include multilevel marketing and franchises. Before advertising your business opportunity or buying into someone else's, you should consult with an attorney experienced in this field of law.

There are numerous opportunities for developing or expanding a thriving business. Each has some potential for success and some risk of failure. Good sense, careful evaluation, and use of skilled professionals will aid you in making an informed decision.

10

Patent Law and Trade Secret Protection

Ordinarily, before a product can achieve a market edge, something must distinguish it from other items in the same general category. Of course, you will want to protect that "something" that sets your product apart so that others cannot exploit its uniqueness. Several bodies of law may help you obtain this protection. The copyright law (discussed in chapter 13) grants to the "author" of an original work in a tangible form the right to prevent others from copying that work. Patent laws allow an inventor the right to prevent others from exploiting a patented invention. Generally speaking, a patent is available for any new and useful process, machine, method of manufacture, "composition of matter," or any new, useful improvement thereof.

Copyright protection is not granted to items of utility. Thus, if a mason produces a decorative carved brick or block for use in an archway, no matter how beautiful, creative, original, or well executed, it is not likely to be protectable under the copyright laws of the United States.

Patent Protection

Such utilitarian objects may, however, be granted protection under the design patent laws; for example, the design of a particular sofa or chair may be granted a design patent though only the aesthetic and not the utilitarian features are protectable. Similarly, a so-called mechanical patent, the one with which you are probably most familiar, may be obtained for any new and unique process, formula, or invention that is a substantial technological innovation. Unfortunately, patents are quite costly and difficult to obtain. It often takes an inordinate period of time for the patent document to be issued, and the period of protection is comparatively short (only twenty years from the date of application).

International Patents

Generally speaking, each country administers its own patent system. The businessperson who wishes to obtain a patent in a foreign country must, therefore, file for patents in that country. One exception to this general rule is the European Patent Regime. A European patent can be filed in any country in Europe although the European Patent Office is located in Munich. Once a European patent is obtained in any member country, the patent can be translated into the language of any other European country and, by filing it in that country, a patent may be obtained in that country without going through another examination process. Americans frequently file their European patents in England so that they can prosecute their patents in the English language.

Trade Secret

Another form of protection, known as trade secret law, allows exploitation of a particular innovation and may afford even greater protection than the copyright or patent laws. A trade secret may be loosely defined as anything that has not been revealed and could give you a competitive advantage. The secret should cover something that you actually use in your business and that you take some reasonable steps to protect. A trade secret may be lost if the owner fails to either identify it or take reasonable steps to protect it. Otherwise, the trade secret protection is perpetual.

Patent or Padlock Dilemma

The determination of whether patent or trade secret protection is most appropriate is sometimes referred to as the "patent or padlock dilemma." It is not sensible to obtain both kinds of protection since achieving one will render the other meaningless. The patent-versus-padlock decision must be made within one year after discovery since the patent laws provide that a patent can be obtained only when the invention in question has not been in public use for more than one year before application is made. Furthermore, use by the inventor for commercial purposes, even in secret, is considered a "public use" within the meaning of the patent law. Thus, during the first year the inventor must decide how the innovation will be protected. If trade secret protection is selected, then patent law is probably lost forever. Selecting a patent is also exclusive and will destroy trade secret protection since the patent application must contain a full description of precisely what was invented. Once issued, *letters patent* will disclose the invention to the public. Thus, it is impossible both to get a patent and to keep some aspect of the invention secret. The patent application is not public information, however, and an applicant may withdraw the application at any time before letters patent are issued without jeopardizing trade secret protection. In order to determine which of these methods of protection should be elected, you should consult an attorney who specializes in intellectual property. See chapter 24, "How to Find a Lawyer and Accountant."

Trade Secret Protection

All that is necessary for something to be protectable as a trade secret is the following:

1. It gives the possessor a competitive advantage
2. It will, in fact, be treated as a secret by you
3. It is not generally known in your industry or business

The fundamental question of trade secret law is, what is protectable? The way you use knowledge and information, the specific portions of information you have grouped together, even the mere assembly of information itself may be a trade secret even if everything you consider important for your secret, is publicly available information. For example, if there are numerous methods for producing a particular dye and you have selected one of them, the mere fact that you have selected this method may itself be a trade secret. The identity of your suppliers may be a trade secret even if they are all listed in the yellow pages. The fact that you have done business with these people and found them to be reputable and responsive to you may make the list of their names a trade secret.

Many trade secrets will be embodied in some form of document. One of the first things you should do is to mark any paper, photograph, or the like, identifying it as confidential. You should also take steps to prevent demonstrations of your trade secret, such as manufacturing methods. Taking these steps will not create trade secret protection, but the fact that an effort has been made to identify the materials and methods you consider secret will aid you in establishing that you treated them as a trade secret should litigation ever occur. In this area, a little thought and cleverness will go a long way toward giving you the protection of the trade secret laws.

First, you should have some degree of physical security. It has been said that physical security is 90 percent common sense and 10 percent true protection. You should restrict the access to the area in which the trade secret is used. Some precaution should be taken to prevent visitors from peering into the manufacturing area where the secret process, formula, or technique is employed. The credentials of delivery and service persons should be examined. The donning of a disguise to gain entry into a restricted area is a favorite ploy of business spies. Employee access to trade secret information should be on a need-to-know basis; employees should not be granted automatic free access to the material you desire to keep as a trade secret.

As noted above, documents, pictures, or sketches containing trade secrets should be clearly labeled. A procedure should be established for controlled employee access to the documents. For instance, one person could be responsible for granting access to them, and a sign-in, sign-out process could be instituted for those permitted access to the documents.

If possible, the information that you consider to be a trade secret should be fragmented. This means no one employee should have possession of the entire secret; thus, no one person will have sufficient information to hurt you. It is also a good idea to have employees sign a confidentiality and non-disclosure agreement when hired. An attorney who deals with intellectual property can prepare form agreements for use within your business.

If it ever becomes important for you to reveal a secret to an outsider, such as when someone desires to purchase the right to exploit your innovation through a licensing arrangement, a different form of confidentiality agreement is in order. These agreements generally provide that in exchange for disclosure of the confidential trade secret information, the party receiving such information will keep it in confidence and will not use it without the express written permission of the person making the disclosure. Again, your intellectual property lawyer can prepare such an agreement for you.

Another method of protecting your trade secret is to engage in some vague labeling. For example, if your trade secret consists of a unique mixture for a glaze, then instead of having the components of the glaze bear their true names, you should label them "Ingredient A," "Ingredient B," "Ingredient C," etc. Then, if an employee quits or if a stranger happens into your office, all they will learn is that by mixing some portion of A with some portion of B, combined with some portion of C, the desired result will be achieved. This will not be very useful information. Similarly, if the trade secret is the temperature at which a glaze is fired, instead of actually marking the thermometer, you may wish to have the original temperature marks removed and replaced by colored zones.

If you are publishing in or contributing to industry or trade journals, take care not to reveal trade secrets. Occasionally, manufacturers or their employees inadvertently disclose valuable information in an attempt to impress their colleagues.

In order to avoid the charge that you are stealing someone else's trade secret, you should question employees who come to work for you from a competitor. If there is any possibility of a new employee using the competitor's trade secret information, the new employee should meet with the former employer and get written permission to use the information while working for you.

Trade secret laws may be the only protection available for your business secrets. Care should therefore be taken to restrict access to the information and to treat the information as truly secret. Contractual arrangements both with employees and outsiders are quite useful. These, coupled with your common sense in the day-to-day operation of your business, will go a long way toward protecting your intellectual property.

Trademarks

11

Many businesspeople manufacture or market products that they wish to have recognized as theirs. This is accomplished by labeling the products with appropriate names, logos, or symbols—commonly known as *trademarks*.

Although modern trademark law is a relatively new development, its historical antecedents date back to medieval England. In those days, certain craft guilds often required members to place their individual marks on the products they produced so that, in the event a product proved defective, the guild could trace its origins to a particular craftsman and impose appropriate sanctions. Thus, the use of marks enabled the guild to maintain the integrity of its name. Moreover, merchants would often affix marks to their products for purposes of identification. Should the product be stolen or misplaced, the merchant could prove ownership by reason of the mark.

The use of marks for purposes of identification would no doubt have worked quite well in an ideal society where all the citizens led principled and moral lives. But such was not the case. It is not particularly surprising that unscrupulous merchants quickly realized that there was easy money to be made from the use of another's mark or one confusingly similar. The shoddy merchants could more readily sell their products by affixing to them the marks belonging to quality manufacturers.

It was in response to this problem of consumer fraud that the first trademark laws developed in the United States. Initially, the emphasis was on prevention of one person passing off his or her product as that of another. In contrast, modern American law focuses upon whether one mark is sufficiently similar to another to cause confusion in the minds of the buying public. The emphasis has, therefore, shifted from the subjective intent of a dishonest manufacturer or merchant passing off goods as those of another to the objective determination of consumer confusion.

Despite this shift, the essential purpose of trademarks and trademark laws has changed little since the days of the craft guilds. Trademarks still function primarily as a means of identifying the source of a particular product. Trademark laws are also designed to enable the trademark proprietor to develop goodwill for the product as well as to prevent another party from exploiting that goodwill—regardless of whether that exploitation is intentional or innocent.

The Need for a Recognizable Mark

What exactly is a trademark? A simplication of the federal definition is: any word, name, symbol, device, or any combination thereof, adopted and used by a person, or which a person has a bona fide intention to use in commerce and subsequently does use, which identifies and distinguishes his or her goods, including a unique product, from those manufactured or sold by others, and indicates the source of those goods, even if that source is unknown.

A trademark owner may be a licensee, broker, or distributor. The term "use in commerce" means the bona fide use of a mark in the ordinary course of trade—not a use made merely to reserve a right in the mark. Reservation of a mark prior to its use can be achieved by filing an intent-to-use application with the Patent and Trademark Office (PTO). The key concept is that the trademark must be *distinguishable*. In order to secure trademark protection, one must devise a distinctive mark.

The most distinctive trademarks are those that are purely arbitrary or fanciful, i.e., those that have no meaning or connotation other than identifying the source of a particular product. For example, the trademark *Kodak* to identify a brand of cameras is purely arbitrary. Less distinctive are trademarks that have another meaning, such as the trademark *Shell* to identify gasoline. Although such trademarks as *Shell* are not purely arbitrary, they are nevertheless afforded substantial protection since the other meaning bears no resemblance to the product identified.

Prohibited Trademarks

Generic and *descriptive* names or marks are not considered distinctive enough to be granted trademark status. A generic trademark merely identifies the product for what it is. Thus, the use of the name *Beer* to identify a brand of beer is generic and would not be accepted as a trademark. Similarly, a descriptive mark only characterizes the attributes or qualities of the product. For example, using the name *Raisin Bran* to identify a cereal is merely descriptive of the product's ingredients and might have difficulty gaining trademark status.

Generic marks are never afforded trademark protection. Descriptive trademarks, however, may be protected in limited circumstances. A descriptive mark may be protected if the proprietor of the mark can prove that it has acquired a *secondary meaning*. Secondary meaning will exist when the public no longer connects the words of the trademark with the literal, dictionary meaning, but rather with a unique product. For example, the descriptive term *TV Guide* also has a secondary meaning as the (registered) trademark of a particular publication that contains television program listings and topical articles about the industry.

In the *Leathersmiths of London* case in the mid-1980s, however, the question was whether the name Leathersmiths of London was a protected trademark. The court held that the word *leathersmith* is generic, at least when used to describe someone who is in the business of working with leather, and, therefore, is not entitled to trademark protection.

Some trademarks, even though they are considered distinctive, are nevertheless prohibited by statute or public policy. Obscene or scandalous trademarks are generally denied trademark protection. Trademarks that are deemed deceptive and misleading, such as the mark *Idaho Potatoes* to identify potatoes produced in some area other than Idaho, are also denied protection.

Protecting a Trademark

Common law is the body of law developed from court decisions rather than from state or federal statutes. Federal or state registration of a trademark has certain advantages but is not necessary. Common-law protection will suffice and has the benefit of not requiring any interaction with governmental agencies.

In order to secure trademark protection, it is not sufficient merely to adopt a distinctive mark. The trademark must be used in the ordinary course of trade, or "used in commerce." The use requirement is fundamental to trademark law and is necessary for common-law protection, as well as federal and state registration. A trademark is deemed to be used when it has been placed in any manner on the product, or its containers or the displays associated with it, or on any of the tags or labels affixed to the product. Thus, it is not always necessary that the trademark actually be physically affixed to the goods. As long as the trademark is associated with the product at the point of sale and in such a way that the product can be readily identified as coming from a particular manufacturer or source, the trademark may be protected.

It should be noted, however, that the mere listing of a trademark in a catalogue, the ordering of labels bearing the trademark, the use of the trademark on invoices, or the exhibition of trademarked goods at a trade show may not be sufficient in and of themselves to constitute use, since the use of the trademark was not associated with the point of sale. To ensure trademark protection, the trademark proprietor would be well advised to physically affix the trademark to the product. In this way, the product is certain to bear the trademark when it is sold.

Common law protects the trademark proprietor against someone else subsequently using a trademark that is confusingly similar. This raises the question of when trademarks are considered confusingly similar. Generally, trademarks will be confusing if they are similar in sound or appearance, particularly if the trademarks are affixed to similar products or if products are marketed throughout the same or similar geographic areas. On the other hand, if two products bearing similar trademarks are not related or are marketed in different geographic areas, there may not be any infringement.

Thus, a business that distributes its products solely in the Northwest could probably adopt and use a trademark already used by a business distributing its product solely in the state of Maine, provided the mark of the Northwest business does not adversely affect the value of the trademark used by the Maine company. Moreover, a Northwest toy manufacturer could probably adopt and use a trademark used by a Northwest chain-saw manufacturer. In these situations, there may be no infringement since it is not likely that the use of the mark by the toy manufacturer would confuse chain-saw purchasers. Here again, appropriation of another's trademark may be wrongful if the use, even by a noncompeting business, would dilute the value of the mark to the original owner. Remedies for trademark infringement will be discussed later in this chapter.

Federal Registration of a Trademark

As noted earlier, the trademark proprietor can procure greater protection under federal or state statutes than under the common law. The federal statute governing trademarks is known as the Lanham Act of 1946. It is not the function of the Lanham Act to grant trademark rights since those are secured by the common-law principles discussed above, but rather to provide a central clearinghouse for existing trademarks via registrations.

In November 1989, the Trademark Law Revision Act (TLRA) of 1988 became effective and made substantive changes to the previous trademark laws. In addition, the trademark law was amended in 1996 to add a federal antidilution provision. Though the Lanham Act provides much of the skeleton of trademark law, these amendments add the needed detail to make trademark law a more complete body of law. It should be noted at the outset that there are two official registers for trademarks, the Principal Register and the Supplemental Register. The following sections on how to register a trademark apply to the Principal Register. A separate section included later in this chapter describes what the Supplemental Register covers and how it may be used.

Prior to enactment of the TLRA, a mark could be registered only upon actual use in interstate commerce. This requirement was satisfied when an applicant sold a few units of the product bearing the trademark in an interstate transaction. A mark could essentially be reserved for later use by making a "token use" at the time of application. The minimum token use requirement allowed the registering of trademarks that might never be used and possibly prevented other proprietors from legitimately using the mark. This judicially sanctioned practice also clogged the federal register with unused marks.

Under the TLRA, token use is no longer permitted. Actual use of the mark is required in order for a trademark to be registered. In addition, the new law allows for the filing of an application for a trademark based on a bona fide intention to use that mark in the future. This reserves and protects a mark for a limited time and to a limited extent prior to its being used in commerce. If the mark is not actually used within a certain time period, the trademark registration will be denied.

Applications Based on Actual Use

The use requirement of the Lanham Act is still in effect for federal trademark protection. This requirement is met if the mark is protected as a common-law trademark. Once the proprietor has established a mark's actual use in commerce, the mark can be registered by filing an application with the Patent and Trademark Office (PTO). This process entails filling out an application, sending in a drawing of the mark, including specimens of the mark used in commerce, and paying the required fee, currently $245. If the examining officer at the PTO accepts the application, the trademark will appear shortly thereafter in the *Official Gazette*. Anyone who believes that he or she would be injured by the issuance of the registration has thirty days to file a written notice stating the reasons for opposition. If nobody objects, or if the objections are found to be without merit, a certificate of registration will be issued.

Applications Based on "Intent to Use"

Under the TLRA, a right to a particular mark can be preserved for future use through the so-called intent-to-use provision. This does not remove the requirement of actual use in commerce, which is still necessary for registration of the mark. Protection of a mark for future use can be accomplished by filing an application based on the applicant's "bona fide intent to use" the mark in commerce. An intent-to-use registration should not be requested merely for the purpose of attempting to reserve a mark. The statute does not explicitly define "bona fide intent," but the good faith of the applicant will be determined from the circumstances surrounding the application and the applicant's conduct with respect to the mark. The history behind the statute's enactment suggests that the applicant's conduct concerning his or her intent to use the mark will be measured against standards accepted in the trade or business.

If the intent-to-use application satisfies the requirements of the PTO regulations, it will receive approval for publication in the *Official Gazette*. Upon such publication, a thirty-day period for opposition to registration of the mark begins to run. This period is similar to that accorded applications for registration of marks that are in actual use. Those applications that go unopposed receive a *notice of allowance*. The date the notice is issued is very important because the reservation of the mark is limited to a period of six months from the date of allowance, during which time actual use of the mark in commerce must begin or the trademark application will lapse.

If an applicant fails to commence using the mark in commerce within the allowable six-month period, it is possible to obtain an extension for another six months. This extension is automatic upon application and payment of fee only if submitted before the original six-month period expires. Four additional six-month extensions are also possible but require, in addition to application and fee submission before expiration of the current six-month period, approval by the PTO upon a showing of good cause why such extension should be granted. In no event shall the period between the date of allowance and the commencement of use of the mark in commerce be permitted to exceed thirty-six months. In making a request for extension, the applicant must include the following:

1. A verified statement of continued bona fide intent to use the mark in commerce
2. Specification as to which classification(s) of goods and services the intent continues to apply
3. Inclusion of the required fee, which is currently $100 per extension, per classification of goods or services

Application forms may be obtained by calling the PTO at (703) 308-0928.

Once actual use of the mark in commerce has occurred, the applicant must file a verified *statement of use*. If everything is in order, the mark will be registered for the goods or services that the statement of use indicates. The Commissioner of the PTO shall notify an applicant as to whether a statement of use has been accepted or refused. An applicant will be allowed to amend the statement of use if the mark was not used on all the goods initially identified.

Constructive Use

An important concept found in the Lanham Act and improved by recent amendments is that of *constructive use*. This concept, which has been called the cornerstone of the intent-to-use method, also applies to use-based applications as well. When an application to register a mark is filed under the doctrine of constructive use, filing constitutes use of the mark as of the filing date. Thus, when the application to register is filed, a right of priority to exclusive use of the mark is created throughout the United States. This is true only if the mark is filed for registration on the Principal Register. The constructive use doctrine does not apply to domestic (or foreign) applications on the Supplemental Register.

This doctrine gives applicants a strong incentive to file for registration as early as possible. The constructive use statute provides priority filing protection and, thereby, prevents others from acquiring the mark by simply using it before the intent-to-use applicant does. Constructive use greatly reduces disputes as to which party has priority, thus saving costs and limiting uncertainty in infringement or opposition proceedings.

Exceptions to the priority right of use are marks used prior to the applicant's filing date, intent-to-use applications filed prior to the applicant's filing date, and use-based applications registered prior to the applicant's filing date. Another exception is applications for registration filed by foreign applicants, if the foreign application was filed prior to the constructive use application.

The new act generally prohibits assignment of intent-to-use applications, thereby preventing applications for marks being filed by individuals for the sole purpose of selling them. However, an intent-to-use application may be assigned to the applicant's business.

Benefits of Registration

First, registration enables a proprietor to use the ® symbol, or the word *trademark*, in conjunction with his or her mark, which may well deter others from using the mark. Proprietors of marks that have not been registered are prohibited from using the above symbols with their marks. Commonly, *TM* for trademark or *SM* for service mark is used in conjunction with an unregistered mark during the application period. These designations have no official status, but they do provide notice to others that the user is claiming a property right in the mark.

Second, registration on the Principal Register is evidence of the validity of the registration, the registrant's ownership of the mark, and the exclusive right to use the mark on identified goods in commerce.

Finally, a registered trademark that has been in continuous use for a period of five consecutive years may become incontestable. By registering the trademark, the proprietor may secure rights superior to those of a prior but unregistered user, but only if the original user does not object to the registrant's use within five years.

Under the trademark law, registration remains in effect for a period of ten years and may be renewed in additional ten-year increments by filing an application for renewal at least six months prior to the expiration of the existing ten-year term. Registrations issued prior to November 16, 1989, received a first-term registration of twenty years. All subsequent registrations are for ten-year renewals. Those registrations that issue from applications filed with the PTO and that were pending as of the effective date of the 1989 amendment have a first term of only ten years, even though filed under the prior law.

The Supplemental Register

Supplemental Register applications may be made directly if the applicant is sure that registration on the Principal Register is unlikely, or in response to the PTO's final refusal to register the mark on the Principal Register. This registration provides protection for individuals capable of distinguishing their marks from those of others, but whose marks do not comply with the requirements for registration on the Principal Register. Marks for the Supplemental Register are not published for, or subject to, opposition. They are, however, published as registered in the *Official Gazette*. If a person believes that he or she will be damaged by the registration of another's mark on the Supplemental Register, that person may, at any time, petition for cancellation of the registration.

Applications filed on the Supplemental Register cannot be based on intent-to-use and do not enjoy the benefits of constructive use. Under the Lanham Act, an application filed on the Supplemental Register had to be in lawful use for a year prior to the filing of the application. For a mark to be eligible for registration on the Supplemental Register under the 1989 amendment, the domestic applicant's mark merely must be in lawful use in commerce, meaning a bona fide use in the ordinary course of trade.

Trademark Loss and Infringement

Loss of Protection

As pointed out above, use or intent to use is a prerequisite to trademark protection. It should be noted that some forms of use might result in the loss of a trademark. A number of well-known trademarks such as *Aspirin*, *Thermos*, and *Escalator* have been lost as a result of improper usage. Trademark protection is lost because the mark is used in some capacity other than as an adjective modifying a noun. When a trademark is used as a noun or a verb, it no longer functions to identify the source of the product, but rather becomes the name of the product itself. At that point, the mark becomes generic and not subject to protection.

Abandonment of a mark will also result in loss of protection. A trademark is deemed "abandoned" when it has not been used for two years and there is no intent to resume its use. Token use will not be sufficient to avoid abandonment. To avoid abandonment, the proprietor does not have to use the mark in interstate commerce in the ordinary course of trade or business, but the mark should be used in intrastate commerce.

Infringement

A trademark that is in use and has been infringed allows the trademark proprietor to sue the infringing party either for monetary damages or for an injunction prohibiting the infringing use, or sometimes for both. Monetary damages may be measured either by the plaintiff's losses resulting from the infringement or by the defendant's profits. In certain exceptional circumstances where the defendant's conduct is willful and flagrant, the plaintiff might also be entitled to exemplary damages equal to three times the actual damages and/or attorney's fees.

The relevant sections under the Lanham Act allow remedies for infringement on marks that actually are in use. This effectively precludes an intent-to-use applicant from suing for infringement because use has not been made of the mark. The law permits anyone who feels that he or she will be damaged by acts that are likely to cause confusion, mistake, or deception as to the origin, sponsorship, or approval of the complainant's goods or services with those of another to sue for unfair competition. Under the act, all remedies available for infringement actions are also available for actions of unfair competition.

Antidilution

In 1996, the federal trademark law was amended to provide special protection to famous marks. The statute does not define "famous mark," though case law likely will. Legislative history suggests that a famous mark is a mark that has been around for a long term and enjoys extensive notoriety.

In the past, it was possible to appropriate a mark for use on goods or services that do not compete with those of the mark's owner so long as there was no likelihood of confusion. As a result, it was possible, for example, to call a dog food *Cadillac,* intending to suggest that it was the elite form of canine fare, despite the fact that the automobile manufacturer Cadillac did not have anything to do with the dog food. The likely intent of the dog food company was to suggest that it was the "Cadillac" of dog foods and thus the top of the line. Under the 1996 amendment, this type of use would probably not be permitted since the dog food's use of the mark *Cadillac* would likely be considered a dilution of the General Motors trademark. While antidilution statutes had been in effect in several states, they were not universal. Now the federal statute will provide protection, at least for famous marks. The remedies available for violations of the antidilution statute are comparable to those that are provided for trademark infringements.

State Registration

Trademarks can also be registered under state law. The trademark proprietor may file with the appropriate state officer a trademark application, along with documentation similar to that required by the Lanham Act. State law protection of a trademark does not extend beyond the borders of the state. The number of specimens of the mark needed to complete registration may vary from state to state, and the registration fee may also be different. Protection under state law can be broader than that found under federal laws. Remedies available under state law are also very likely to be different from those found under the federal statute. If a conflict arises between federal and state trademark law, it is important to remember that under the supremacy clause of the U.S. Constitution, federal law will supercede state law.

Conclusion

Obviously, registration can be quite beneficial to a manufacturer who has invested time, money, and energy in developing a reputation for quality work. Procuring trademark protection on either the state or federal level may require a considerable amount of time and skill. In this regard, an attorney may prove invaluable. An attorney can, first of all, determine if the benefits to be derived from registration justify the expenses. The total cost of trademark registration usually runs about $1000, not counting any artist's fees for drawings. Second, an attorney can research a trademark index to determine if there are any conflicting marks. Finally, an attorney can complete the application and deal with any problems that may occur while it is being processed for registration.

If you are interested in contacting attorneys who specialize in trademark work, you can consult the yellow pages of the telephone directory (look under intellectual property lawyers or patent attorneys), or ask your state bar association for some recommendations.

12

Copyrights

It is quite common for start-up companies to use literature, computer software, videotapes, artwork, and similar material created by others. This material may be protected by the copyright law, and its unauthorized use may subject the user to liability for copyright infringement. There are, however, some situations in which you may be able to use another's work without obtaining permission. The guidelines for this use are found in the federal copyright law.

Some businesses develop their own copyrightable brochures, advertising copy, catalogs, posters, and the like, and since businesspeople tend to take a proprietary view of their creations, they may wish to prevent others from using their work without permission. Again, the copyright law provides the vehicle by which these works may be protected. In this chapter, I will discuss some significant portions of the copyright law and their possible application to your business.

Copyright law in the United States has its foundation in

the Constitution, which provides in Article I, Section 8, that Congress shall have the power "to promote the progress of science and useful arts, by securing for limited time to authors and inventors the exclusive right to their respective writings and discoveries." The first Congress exercised this power and enacted a copyright law. The legislation was periodically revised by later Congresses until 1909. No major changes were made in the law from 1909 until the Copyright Revision Act of 1976.

Prior to enactment of the 1976 law, unpublished works were protected by common-law copyright governed by state laws. This protection could vary considerably from state to state. Federal protection under the 1909 act began by protecting a published work to which a copyright notice was attached. The Copyright Revision Act of 1976 preempts the field of copyright law—in other words, it is now the only legislation generally governing copyright. This law was significantly amended once again in 1989 when the United States became a party to the international copyright treaty known as the Berne Convention.

Publication within the context of copyright law is a technical term that applies to all copyrightable material. Under the old law, it meant an unrestricted public display. Today, publication is defined as "the distribution of copies of a work to the public by sale or other transfer of ownership, or by rental, lease, or loan."

The new law became effective on January 1, 1978, but it is not retroactive. Thus, works created by the same person before and after January 1, 1978, will be covered by copyright laws that have some fundamentally different provisions. It is important to be aware of the basic differences and aware of which law applies to a particular work. Works created and sold prior to January 1, 1978, will be governed by the provisions of the old act. Works created, but not publicly displayed or offered for sale prior to January 1, 1978, are governed by the new law. What difference does it make? In many cases, it determines who owns the copyright in the work—the creator or the purchaser.

What Can Be Copyrighted

The Constitution permits Congress to provide protection for a limited time to "authors" for their "writings." An author, from the point of view of copyright law, is a creator—be it a photographer, sculptor, writer, computer programmer. Congress avoided the use of the word *writings* in describing the scope of copyright protection. Instead, it grants copyright protection to "original works of authorship fixed in any tangible medium of expression." Legislative comments on this section of the act suggest that Congress chose to use this wording rather than term *writings* in order to have more leeway to legislate in the copyright field. There have been debates over what constitutes a writing, but it is now clear from a 1980 amendment to the act that the term *author* includes the creator of computer software programs.

The 1976 act expressly exempts from copyright protection "any idea, procedure, process, system, method of operation, concept, principle, or discovery." In short, a copyright extends only to the "expression" of creations of the mind, not to the ideas themselves. Frequently, no clear line of division between an idea and its expression exists. For now, it is sufficient to note that a pure idea, such as a plan to create an innovative advertising program, cannot be copyrighted—no matter how original or creative that idea is.

The law and the courts generally avoid using the copyright law to arbitrate the public's taste. Thus, a work can be copyrighted even if it makes no pretense to aesthetic or academic merit. The only requirements are that a work be original and show some creativity. Originality—as distinguished from uniqueness—requires that a work be created independently. Originality, however, does not require that it be the only one of its kind. For example, cartographers who independently create identical maps are each entitled to copyright protection. Because their works often look similar to untrained observers, many cartographers will include an intentional minor error on a map so that if the identical error appears on another map alleged to have been independently created, this minor error will provide obvious evidence of copying. In writing this book, I have intentionally included typographical errors to inhibit copyright infringement.

Scope of Protection

A copyright is actually a collection of five exclusive rights. First is *the right to reproduce a work by any means*. The scope of this right can be hard to define, especially when it involves works such as photocopying, microfilm, or videotape. Under the Copyright Act of 1976, someone may reproduce protected works without permission only if such reproduction involves either a fair or an exempted use as defined by the act (explained later in this chapter).

Second is *the right to prepare derivative works based on a copyrighted work*. A derivative work is one that transforms or adapts the subject matter of one or more preexisting works.

Third is *the right to distribute copies to the public for sale or lease*. However, once a person sells a copyrighted work or permits uncontrolled distribution, the right to control further uses of that work usually ends. This is known as the "first sale" doctrine; it does not apply if the work is merely in the possession of someone else temporarily by virtue of bailment, rental, lease, license, or loan. In these instances, the copyright owner retains the right to control the further sale or other disposition of the work. Moreover, the first-sale doctrine does not apply if the copyright owner has a contract with the purchaser restricting the purchaser's freedom to use the work, as is the case with many software programs. In such a case, if the purchaser exceeds the restrictions, he or she may incur liability. In this situation, however, the copyright owner's remedy will be governed by contract law rather than by copyright law.

One should distinguish between a sale of a work and a sale of the copyright in that work. If nothing is said about the copyright when the work is sold, the seller retains the copyright. Since purchasers may not be aware of this, a seller may wish to call it to their attention either in the sales memorandum or on the work itself. If a license is granted, it should be in writing and should be very specific in the scope of rights being granted. For example, may a person who has purchased a license to videotapes of a lecture also market the copyrighted instruction manual used in conjunction with the lecture? Generally the answer is no, but the drafter of the license should be clear in defining the boundaries of permissible uses.

Fourth is *the right to perform the work publicly*, such as to broadcast a film on television or to show it in a lecture room or meeting room.

Fifth is *the right to display the work publicly*. Once the copyright owner has sold a copy of the work, however, the purchaser has the right to display that copy but is generally still prohibited from reproducing it.

These rights are divisible, which means they can be transferred in whole or in part. If the copyright owner takes no special action upon selling the work, he or she is presumed to have retained all rights. If desired, however, the copyright owner may explicitly transfer any one or more of these rights.

Ownership of Copyright

As a general rule, the creator of a work owns the copyright. The person who owns the copyright also automatically owns the exclusive rights. Under the old law, when a work was sold, ownership of a common-law (prepublication) copyright passed to the purchaser unless the creator reserved the copyright in a written agreement. In other words, there was a presumption in the law that a sale included the work itself plus all rights in that work.

The Copyright Act of 1976, as amended, reversed the presumption that the sale of a work carries the copyright with it. Today, unless there is a written agreement to the contrary, the creator retains the copyright when the work is sold.

The creators of a *joint work* are co-owners of the copyright in the work. A joint work is defined as "a work prepared by two or more authors with the intention that their contributions be merged into inseparable or interdependent parts of a unitary whole." Thus, whatever profit one creator makes from use of the work must be shared equally with the others unless they have a written agreement that states otherwise.

The key point is the intent that the parts be absorbed or combined into an integrated unit at the time the work is created. The late Professor Melville Nimmer of UCLA Law School commented that although such an intent must exist at the time the work is created, not at a later date, the authors do not necessarily have to work together, work during the same period, or even know each other. However, the joint works definition does not include the situation where an artist creates a work such as a piano solo, not intending that the work involve another artist, and later commissions lyrics. If there is no intention to create a unitary or indivisible work, each creator may own the copyright to that creator's individual contribution.

In *Ashton-Tate Corp. v. Ross,* the Ninth Circuit Court of Appeals held that joint authorship was not established by the mere contribution of ideas and guidance for the user interface of a computer spreadsheet because the joint authorship requires each author to make an independently copyrightable contribution.

Works for Hire

Works considered to be *works for hire* are an important exception to the general rule that a person owns the copyright in a work he or she has created. If a work was created by an employee on the job, the law considers the product a work for hire, and the employer will own the copyright. However, the parties can avoid the application of this rule with a well-written contract. If the employment contract states that creating the copyrightable material in question is not part of the "scope of employment," the employee retains the copyright, and the creation is not a work for hire.

A work for hire is defined as "a work made by an employee within the scope of his or her employment." The principle has been based on the following grounds:

1. The work is produced on behalf of and under the direction of the employer
2. The employee is paid for the work
3. The employer, having paid all the costs and bearing all the risks of loss, should reap any gain

Courts also consider the amount of an employer's artistic advice before, during, and after the work was created to determine whether the creator is working for hire or as an independent contractor.

Some courts developed a doctrine whereby an independent contractor was considered to be a "special employee" for copyright purposes when a commissioning party had the right to exercise control over the work. This resulted in the commissioning party owning the copyright rather than the independent contractor. In 1989, the U.S. Supreme Court, in *Community for Creative Non-Violence (CCNV) v. Reid,* held that unless the party creating the work is an actual employee as that term is defined in the law, the copyright will belong to the creator rather than to the commissioning party. The court left open the question of whether the work could be considered a joint work by virtue of the party's intent.

If the creator is an independent contractor, the works will only be considered works for hire when:

1. The parties have signed a written agreement to that effect, and
2. The work is specially ordered or commissioned as a contribution to a collective work, a supplementary work (one that introduces, revises, comments upon, or assists a work by another), a compilation, an instructional text, answer material for a test or the test itself, an atlas, motion picture, or an audiovisual work

Thus, unless there is a contractual agreement to the contrary, the independent contractor owns the copyright.

Derivative Works

In the case of a *derivative work,* the contributing author owns only what that person contributed. A derivative work is defined (in 17 U.S.C. Section 101) as:

> A work based upon one or more preexisting works, such as translation, fictionalization, motion picture version, sound recording, art reproduction, abridgment, condensation, or any other form in which a work may be recast, transformed, or adapted. A work consisting of editorial revisions, annotations, elaborations, or other modifications which, as a whole, represent an original work of authorship, is a "derivative work."

Thus, any work based completely or substantially upon a preexisting work, if it satisfies the originality requirement and is not itself an infringing work, will be separately copyrightable. The distinction between a derivative work and a joint work lies in the intent of each contributor at the time the contribution is created. If the work is created with the intention that the contributions be merged into inseparable or interdependent parts of a "unitary whole," then the merger creates a joint work. If such intention occurs only after the work has been created, then the merger results in a derivative or collective work.

Collective Works

A *collective work* is defined (in 17 U.S.C. Section 101) as "a work, such as a periodical issue, anthology, or encyclopedia, in which a number of contributions, constituting separate and independent works in themselves, are assembled into a collective whole."

The originality involved in a collective work is the collection and assembling of preexisting works, which may themselves be copyrightable, without any internal changes in such material. This assemblage of works is copyrightable.

Copyright Protection for Utilitarian Objects

Because copyright law was originally intended to protect literary works, earlier versions of the law omitted protection for three-dimensional designs. These designs were not given copyright protection until 1870.

The Copyright Act of 1909 did not contain any protection for utilitarian objects, but the regulations adopted to interpret the law extended copyright protection to the artistic elements of a utilitarian piece. The regulation stated that the aesthetic, but not mechanical or utilitarian, aspects of the item would be protected.

Despite the lack of specific legislation, some protection is available for manufacturers of utilitarian objects. The copyright law may be relied on to a limited extent. For example, if an individual draws a copyrightable picture and obtains copyright protection for that design, then the copyrighted picture could be used or incorporated into any utilitarian item and be protected.

Notice Requirement

The requirement that original works and all copies have a copyright notice affixed to them on publication is basic to both the Copyright Act of 1909 and the Copyright Revision Act of 1976. The notice consists of the international symbol © or the word *copyright* or its abbreviation *Copr.,* the name of the author (in the case of works for hire, this is usually the employer), and the year of first publication. For example:

Copyright 2000 by John Doe

or

© John Doe, 2000

The order of the words is unimportant.

Under the Copyright Act of 1909, a publication without notice caused the work to fall into the public domain, and once the rights were lost, they could not be retrieved. It was publication with notice that created a federal copyright under this law.

Under the Copyright Revision Act of 1976, a federal copyright is created as soon as an original work is made in tangible form. Until 1989, however, the proper notice had to be attached at publication if you wished to retain a federal copyright after publication. However, a savings clause was added. Section 405 now provides that a copyright is not invalidated by publication without copyright notice under any of the following circumstances:

1. The notice is omitted from a small number of copies distributed to the public
2. The work is registered within five years of publication and a reasonable effort is made to add the notice to all works distributed in the United States after the omission is discovered
3. The notice was omitted, intentionally or otherwise, in violation of an express written agreement that distributed copies would bear the required notice

The Copyright Office has indicated that the savings provision of the law may not be used if there has been an intentional omission of the copyright notice by the person claiming copyright protection, though in at least one case an individual was allowed to use the savings provision where there had been an intentional omission of the notice.

After the 1989 amendment to the 1976 act, notice is not required on works created or first published after March 1, 1989. Although notice is not required on works published after March 1, 1989, notice should still be used even today to make others aware of your rights. One who copies a work, believing it to be in the public domain because there is no notice, is considered an *innocent* infringer. In this situation, the author whose work is copied cannot recover damages. In fact, the court might even allow the copier to continue using the work. The 1989 amendment provides that if notice is used, an infringer cannot then claim that the infringement was innocent.

Filing an Application and Depositing the Work

To register a copyright you must *file* an application form with the Copyright Register, Library of Congress, Washington, D.C. 20559. You must also *deposit* two copies of the work. Remember, if you have a copyright notice on your work, or if your work was published after March 1, 1989, even without a notice, you already have a copyright. Under the Copyright Revision Act of 1976, as amended, registration is necessary *only*:

1. As a prerequisite to commencing an infringement action
2. When the copyright owner wishes to take advantage of the savings provision of Section 405
3. If the Register of Copyrights demands registration of published works bearing a copyright notice (which is not likely to happen unless you have been in correspondence with that office)

The current law separates registration from the deposit requirements. Under the 1909 act, registration involved filing a copyright application, paying a $6 fee *and* depositing two copies of the work itself or two photographs of the original. However, fine prints came within the requirements of actual copies, making it necessary to deposit two actual prints. Congress recognized the economic hardship this caused artists and the fact that many of them intentionally failed to take advantage of copyright protection because of the burdensome deposit requirement and, therefore, modified it. Now, the

Register of Copyrights is allowed to exempt certain categories from the deposit requirement or provide for alternative forms of deposit. This has been done in the case of computer software, films, videotapes, and other items.

Under the present law, you should deposit two of the "best" copies of the work with the Library of Congress within three months of publication. If the objects are bulky, fragile, or valuable, photographs may be deposited instead of the actual work. The same photograph privilege applies to fine prints in editions of three hundred or fewer. Filing the application (which includes a $20 fee) need not be done at the time of deposit. When you feel depositing two copies is a hardship, you may apply for a waiver of the two-copy deposit requirement.

Although you can delay registration, there are at least two reasons why you should deposit the work and register the copyright (i.e., file the application) within three months of publication. First, the copyright law prohibits the awarding of attorney's fees and statutory damages for infringements that occur before registration, unless registration took place within three months of publication. Second, if you deposit the required two copies of the work within three months but postpone sending the registration form and fee, the Copyright Office will require two more copies of the work when you eventually do send in the form and money. Finally, if the two copies are not deposited within the requisite three-month period, the Register of Copyrights may demand them. If the copies are not submitted within three months after demand, the person upon whom demand was made may be subject to a fine of up to $250 for each unsubmitted work. In addition, such person or persons may be required to pay the Library of Congress an amount equal to the retail cost of the work. If no retail cost has been established, the costs incurred by the Library in acquiring the work, provided such costs are reasonable, will be substituted. The copyright proprietor who willfully and repeatedly refuses to comply with such a demand may be liable for an additional fine of $2,500.

Period of Protection

The Copyright Act of 1909 granted copyright protection in a work for a twenty-eight-year period, which could be renewed for one additional twenty-eight-year period. Under the revised law, a work created on or after January 1, 1978, has copyright protection from the instant it is fixed in tangible form until fifty years after the creator's death. If the work was created jointly, the copyright expires fifty years after the last author dies. There are no renewals for copyrights created under the 1976 act. Copyrights granted under the 1909 act that were in effect on January 1, 1978, will automatically receive an extension to create a term of seventy-five years from the date the copyright was first obtained. It is important to note that this automatic extension applies only to copyrights that were in effect on January 1, 1978. Thus, if the copyright on a work had lapsed prior to January 1, 1978, the copyright will not be revived. In all cases, copyright terms end on December 31 of the given year.

The copyright period of life plus fifty years applies only to works created by human beings using their own names. In other cases, for example, a corporation that obtains a copyright in accordance with the doctrine of works for hire, or for works created anonymously or pseudonymously, the period of protection is either one hundred years from creation or seventy-five years from first publication, whichever expires first.

Infringement

The federal courts have exclusive jurisdiction over copyright infringement litigation. Under both the 1909 and 1976 acts, the trial judge has wide discretion in setting damages. Under the 1909 act, a judge could award either actual damages (plaintiff's out-of-pocket losses or defendant's profit) or statutory damages. Under the 1976 act, as amended in 1989, a judge may also award actual damages, and the range of statutory damages is greater: as little as $200 for innocent infringement, between $500 and $20,000 for the typical case, and up to $100,000 for willful infringement. Both acts allow the awarding of reasonable attorney's fees to the prevailing party. Both acts also provide for injunctions against continued infringement and, in some cases, impoundment. The statute of limitations for both acts allows a plaintiff three years to file a lawsuit after the infringement occurs. This time frame refers to the date the infringement was committed, not the date the infringement was discovered.

In the case of willful infringement for commercial gain, criminal sanctions may also be imposed. The law was amended in 1982 to provide more severe penalties for those who unlawfully reproduce and sell sound recordings, motion pictures, audiovisual works, or phonorecords. Under these provisions, a criminal infringer may receive up to five years imprisonment and/or a fine of up to $250,000.

Fair Use

Not every copying of a protected work is an infringement. There are two basic types of noninfringing use: *fair use* and *exempted use*.

The Copyright Act of 1976 recognizes that copies of a protected work "for purposes such as criticism, comment, news reporting, teaching (including multiple copies for classroom use), scholarship or research" can be considered fair use and, therefore, not an infringement. However, this is not a complete list, nor is it intended as a definition of fair use. In addition, the act cites four criteria to be considered in determining whether a particular use is or is not fair:

1. The purpose and character of the use, including whether it is for commercial use or nonprofit educational purposes
2. The nature of the copyrighted work
3. The amount and substantiality of the portion used in relation to the copyrighted work as a whole
4. The effect of the use upon the potential market for, or value of, the copyrighted work

The act does not rank these four criteria, nor does it exclude other factors in determining the question of fair use. In effect, all that the act does is leave the doctrine of fair use to be developed by the courts.

The U.S. Supreme Court has interpreted the scope of the fair use doctrine in connection with motion pictures. In *Universal Studios, et al. v. Sony Corporation, et al.*, which the Supreme Court decided in 1984, the plaintiff movie producers claimed that the defendant, Sony Corporation, was enabling consumers to violate the plaintiff's copyright by selling a machine that could make off-the-air copies of the plaintiff's copyrighted works. This activity, it was alleged, should subject the defendants to liability for copyright infringement as both facilitator and conspirator. The Supreme Court rejected this contention and held that the copying of copyrighted works in one's own home for noncommercial purposes was fair use, at least when applied to audiovisual works. The majority of the justices expressly refrained from considering the applicability of this doctrine to any other forms of copyrighted works.

In *American Geophysical Union v. Texaco, Inc.,* the U.S. Court of Appeals for the Second Circuit held that making even one copy of a copyrighted professional journal for purposes of retaining an article in one's file for reference purposes was an infringement. The court pointed out that if the employees of the Texaco research lab desired additional copies of articles in the copyrighted journals, reprints could have been purchased. The making of an unauthorized copy deprived the copyright owner of a sale and was, therefore, an infringement.

It has also been held that the mere fact that permission to quote from a copyrighted work has been requested and denied does not necessarily mean that a use will be infringing. In *Maxtone-Graham v. Burtchaell,* the defendant, a Catholic priest, requested permission to quote from the plaintiff's book of interviews with women who were, as the title suggests, *Pregnant by Mistake*. Since the priest's intended use of the quoted material was to support his "pro-life" publication, permission was denied. He, nevertheless, used the excerpts. In the resulting litigation, the court held that the use was "fair" since the priest's unauthorized use of the copyrighted material was a "productive" use, and since the plaintiff was not necessarily deprived of sales.

It is, therefore, still relatively unclear how broad or narrow the scope of the fair use doctrine really is.

In many instances, the ambiguities of the fair use doctrine are resolved by statutory exemptions. The exempted uses apply to situations where the public interest in making a copy outweighs the potential harm to the copyright proprietor. For example, the library and archives exemption allows libraries and archives to reproduce and distribute a single copy of a work provided that certain requirements are met. However, this exemption in no way affects the applicability of fair use, nor does it apply where such copying is prohibited in contractual arrangements agreed to by the library or archive when it acquired the work.

Getting Information and Forms

If you desire more information, write to the Copyright Office, Library of Congress, Washington, D.C. 20559, and ask for a free copyright information packet.

13

Licensing

Once you have obtained one or more forms of intellectual property protection—trademark, trade dress (discussed in chapter 14), patent, or copyright—you may exploit your creations and prevent others from interfering with your rights. For instance, you may convert pictures from your copyrighted catalog into posters and sell them.

If another company likes your work and wishes to duplicate it, you can exploit your own intellectual property by granting the other person a *license*.

A license to use your copyright, trademark, trade dress, or patent should be in writing. It should describe the scope of the user's permission, such as how long the license will last, whether the user can market copies throughout the world or only in specific locations, and whether the license allows exploitation of the entire intellectual property or only a portion of it (e.g., use of a copyrighted photo on T-shirts only, but not on anything else). Care should be taken when defining these boundaries. If a U.S. license permits sales or other exploitation of the licensed products or technology in, for example, Canada, then Canadian sales to a business that ships the goods to the United States may be within the scope of permitted use, resulting in the U.S. licenses competing with Canadian licenses for sales within the U.S. This "gray market" problem can be controlled by using care in drafting the license agreement.

Skilled drafters will avoid ambiguity in language such as "American" when intending the United States, since all countries in the North and South Americas may be considered "American."

Care should also be taken to avoid allowing your intellectual property to be exploited in countries that do not honor U.S. intellectual property laws, that have laws that are less protective than ours, or that have no intellectual property law at all. The U.S. State Department has a "watch list" of countries that do not honor their intellectual property treaty obligations or that have a poor record of enforcement with respect to intellectual property. The advent of the World Wide Web has presented a myriad of new challenges. Since material may be captured anywhere in the world, even in areas that may not be desirable, care should be taken in determining what is placed on the Web and whether your license permits or prohibits Web postings.

Whether Licensing Is the Proper Choice

Several issues should be considered before deciding whether to grant a license. The factors that follow may influence your decision to license or not, but by no means is this intended to be an exhaustive list.

First, the nature of the work, technology, etc., must be considered. If the property rights to be licensed are in a new technology that is susceptible to rapid change (e.g., a new development in the computer or electronic industry), or a product that is simply one of many alternatives on the market, then the value of the license to the potential licensee will be decreased. The licensee may then require that updated product enhancements be provided as part of the license agreement. On the other hand, if the product is a new development that exists without alternatives and is thereby likely to afford the licensee a greater period of exploitation, the licensor is in a much stronger negotiating position to demand a higher price.

Another issue to consider is whether or not the licensee will be permitted to sublicense. When permitted, the right to sublicense can affect the price paid for a license. In the area of computer software, for instance, sublicense rights are often part of the licensee's comprehensive business plan. Sublicense provisions should be carefully drafted and tied directly to the terms of the original license agreement. All ownership of the licensor's technology should be retained by the licensor via specific provisions in the original license agreement. Provisions should be made for quality-control checks of the licensed technology. All provisions in the original license agreement should be drafted to apply to any sublicense agreements negotiated by the licensee.

If the licensor is considering licensing a patented technology, the safety of the technology and potential for liability arising from its use should be evaluated. Licenses can be drafted with "exculpatory" clauses in which the licensee agrees to assume all liability arising from the use of the licensed technology. Exculpatory clauses that deal with latent design defects (i.e., defects not readily discoverable), however, may not entirely insulate the licensor from liability. Careful testing of the technology to ensure removal of defects will reduce the risk of such a situation occurring. The exculpatory clause itself, by careful enumeration of what liabilities the licensee assumes, can also provide extra protection to the licensor. The exculpatory clause should be written by an attorney experienced in drafting this type of provision.

Method of Payment

Once the decision to license has been made, the price must be negotiated. Payment for the license should be spelled out in the license document. You can demand a flat fee in exchange for permission to use your copyright material, trademark, or patent, or you may prefer to receive some portion of the income as a royalty. This payment can either be a fixed amount per item or a percentage, perhaps 5 percent, of the money received by the person exploiting the right. Care should be taken to define quite specifically the sum upon which the percentage will be based. Specify, for example, if it will be a percentage of the net or gross receipts from the sale of items covered by the license, and carefully define the term used.

Payments based on sales are referred to as *royalties*. One should be very careful to define when they are due and payable and on what basis they are to be calculated. Unfortunately, numerous unscrupulous individuals have used creative accounting to reduce their obligations. In the case of *Buchwald v. Paramount Studios,* Art Buchwald established that he, and not Eddie Murphy, was responsible for the treatment that ultimately became the movie *Coming to America.* Pursuant to his contract with Paramount, Buchwald was to receive "a share of net profits." As of the date of trial, the movie had grossed $350 million, but by the use of creative accounting, Paramount alleged a net *loss* of $18 million on the picture. The poorly drafted, one-sided contract deprived Buchwald of his fair share of the movie's earnings. While Buchwald was successful in his challenge, this case underscores the importance of drafting unambiguous royalty arrangements.

If international transactions are involved, be sure to specify which country's currency is to be used. The value of U.S. dollars, Canadian dollars, and Australian dollars for example, typically differ, and there is a cost involved in currency conversion.

It is also important to include in a licensing agreement a provision whereby you can verify the accuracy of the records showing what is due to you. This can be accomplished by requiring the person to whom the license is granted to have an accounting report preceding or accompanying any royalty checks. If you dispute the validity of the report, there should be an agreed-upon right to have an independent accountant audit the books. Some of my more confident clients have agreed to provisions that place the obligation for paying the outside accountant on the party rendering the accounting if an error of more than 10 percent of the total payment is discovered.

Acknowledgment of Intellectual Property Owner; Quality of Reproductions

In order to retain the protection afforded by the patent, trademark, or copyright laws, you must require any person who uses your creation to acknowledge your ownership and include the appropriate notice on the work.

It is common to see a legend that states, for example, "Reproduced with permission of J. Jones, the copyright owner."

Since the work marketed after you have granted a license will bear your name or trademark, it will usually be difficult, if not impossible, for consumers to distinguish between your work and those works reproduced by the person to whom you have granted a license. For this reason, it is important for you to retain some degree of quality control over the licensed product. In fact, trademark law requires quality control, and it has been held that a "naked" license, which is one without quality control measures, is void. A provision in the license should, therefore, require the licensee to demonstrate some method by which the item will be reproduced and some means by which you can evaluate the quality of the final products. To cite a grand example, when the Metropolitan Museum of Art in New York City obtained the right to create copies of some of the pieces displayed in the King Tut exhibit, one of the primary concerns of the Egyptian government was the quality of the reproductions.

In order for the license to be valid and enforceable, both parties should sign it. You should make it clear that the license is personal and may not be assigned or exploited by anybody but the person to whom it is given unless you give your written permission. It is also wise to provide that the license is void and no longer in effect if any of its terms, including payment of royalties, are violated.

Lawyers who specialize in intellectual property can be helpful in explaining the numerous options available to you through the licensing process. They can be helpful in drafting a document that will afford you maximum protection while another person exploits your intellectual property. It is also important to record your license in the appropriate place—the Copyright Office or the office of the Commissioner of Patents and Trademarks—when such recording is available. An intellectual property lawyer should assist you with this process.

14

Advertising

There are a host of different issues that arise in the context of advertising. In chapter 11, I discussed the method by which you may protect your product name and logo. The copyright protection available for business literature, ads, and posters was considered in chapter 12. In this chapter, I will discuss several other important legal considerations that may arise when planning an advertising program.

Government Regulation

To begin with, a business may always tout the qualities of its products or services, but those representations must be true. If there are any misrepresentations contained in ads or promotions, the state or federal government may file a lawsuit to redress this wrong.

Most states have consumer protection laws which, among other things, impose fines and other legal sanctions on businesses that engage in misleading advertising. The state attorney general can cause an offending advertisement to be withdrawn. Similarly, the Federal Trade Commission is involved in policing businesses that are engaged in interstate commerce. If your business activity extends beyond your state boundaries and either touches or affects another state, then the Federal Trade Commission has jurisdiction over your company.

If the product or service that your business provides has any medicinal benefits, then it must first be approved by the Food and Drug Administration. The approval process is quite technical and will require you to work closely with a lawyer specializing in this area of practice. Failure to comply with the requirements of the Food and Drug Administration could subject you to fines and, in some instances, imprisonment.

Comparative Advertising

It has become quite common for businesses to boost the merits of their products and services by comparing them with those of their competitors. This form of comparative advertising is permissible provided that the statements made are true. Thus, a business would be permitted to use the name of a competitor and describe the competitor's products in an ad, even though the comparison will likely point out the competing product's or service's inferiority, as long as there is no likelihood that a consumer would believe the advertiser is also selling the competing product or service and as long as the statements made are accurate. In a leading case, it was held permissible to use the names of famous perfumes in an ad that stated that those who like the famous perfume will also like the advertiser's less expensive product. The court felt that there was no possibility of a consumer being confused into believing that the expensive perfume manufacturer was advertising for the cheaper knockoff scent. In addition, since the perfume smelled the same, the statements made were felt to be accurate.

A closely related situation arises when one makes disparaging remarks about the product of another. In this situation, the one who intentionally or negligently makes untrue disparaging remarks about the product or service of another business may be held legally accountable to the injured party. In a landmark case where a famous art critic stated that a particular painting was a forgery and the sale of that painting fell through, the critic was sued successfully for the painting owner's lost profits. It should be noted that for a disparaging remark to be actionable, it must be both untrue and believed by a reasonable person. If the statement made was so outlandish as to be unbelievable, it is unlikely the owner whose product was disparaged will be able to prove any injury. Thus, if a car manufacturer claimed its competitor's vehicle was so poorly constructed that it literally fell apart within the first week of use, the likelihood is that this gross exaggeration would not be believed and, therefore, would not be actionable.

Publicity and Privacy

A company may use a celebrity to endorse its product, provided the celebrity consents to the endorsement. If not, the company may be liable to the celebrity for violating his or her right of publicity. This right is granted to those who commercially exploit their names, voices, or images, such as actors or singers. The use of a look-alike for commercial purposes may be actionable. Thus, when manufacturers used look-alikes for Jackie Onassis, Woody Allen, and the rap group The Fat Boys, liability was imposed.

People who have not achieved notoriety because of their commercial activities may have a right of privacy, and, thus, a claim, if their names or likenesses are used in an advertisement without their permission. In one curious case, a bank photographed several employees engaged in their day-to-day work. These pictures were displayed as part of the bank's promotional material for a trade show. When the employees were given the day off to see the trade show and saw their photos, they retained an attorney who filed suit. One might conclude from this case that it is dangerous to give employees a day off so that they can attend trade shows. A more prudent conclusion, however, would be that even bank employees who are not entertainers must grant permission for their names, voices or likenesses to be used for advertising purposes.

If an individual's photograph is not the focal point of the ad, but rather is merely an incidental part, such as a head in a crowd or a member of an audience, then an individual's permission may not be essential before the photograph can be used commercially. Even though you may not be required to have permission from an individual before using his or her photograph, it is probably a good idea to get a signed photo release whenever possible. The release should be worded in such a way as to give your business permission to use the name and likeness or, where relevant, the person's voice, for any and all purposes, including advertising your business. This will protect you if, for example, the individual ultimately becomes popular and you wish to use the photos you obtained at an earlier date before the individual became a celebrity.

Unauthorized Use of Trademark

An advertiser may be permitted to use the name or logo of another business in its ad as long as there is no likelihood that the average viewer would believe that the ad was sponsored by the company whose name or logo you are casually using. In other words, as long as there is no likelihood of confusion between your product and the name and logo belonging to another, you may use the other's trademark. For example, it would be permissible for you to have an ad for a baseball team contain a photo of individuals incidentally holding a distinctively shaped Coca-Cola bottle, as long as it is clear from the advertisement that the soft drink manufacturer is not sponsoring the ad. Similarly, an automobile advertisement may show the vehicle streaking through a metropolitan area and passing several famous businesses.

Geographic Locations

Geographic locations may also be used in advertisements without obtaining the owner's consent. It would be permissible for a company to advertise its product by having someone stand in front of a famous building, such as the Empire State Building or the World Trade Center. Since items of utility are not copyrightable, buildings, parks, and other landmarks are not protectable under the copyright laws and, thus, may incidentally be used in advertising programs without the owner's permission. In one case, however, it was held that a building that was architecturally unique, identifiable, and famous could enjoy the protection of the trade dress laws when it was prominently featured on a poster. Perhaps the distinction between an incidental use of a building as a backdrop and focusing on the prominent identifiable architectural features of a building is significant.

Trade Dress

A form of advertising that has been given special protection is package design. While it is true that the copyright laws do not protect functional items, such as product packaging, the courts have developed a form of protection known as *trade dress*. This means that the design elements of a particular packaging design are protectable as long as they are not otherwise functional, e.g., a hanger or a lid. The trade dress form of protection may be automatic and has been extended beyond traditional packaging.

A leading case involved Blue Mountain Greeting Card Co., which had developed a distinct and very identifiable line of greeting cards. These cards had become quite well known and commercially successful. The Hallmark Greeting Card Company realized this fact and designed a line of cards that were not identical to those of Blue Mountain but, in essence, appropriated the Blue Mountain "look and feel." Consumers seeing the Hallmark cards would reasonably believe that they were merely an extension by Blue Mountain of its popular line. For this reason, the court held Hallmark liable for infringing Blue Mountain's trade dress in the cards.

The U.S. Supreme Court, in 1992, endorsed the expansion of the trade dress doctrine in *Two Pesos v. Taco Cabana*. In this case, the court stated that the nonfunctional aspects of a business might be protectable trade dress provided they are distinctive and identifiable. The fast-food restaurant's architectural features, décor, and menu, may be protected so long as they have a distinctive "look and feel," are not functional, and have achieved "notoriety." Thus, it is likely that McDonald's "golden arches" would be considered protectable trade dress. The trade dress doctrine has been used to prevent copying of a business's distinctive theme, a food company's packaging, and a jewelry manufacturer's earring backers.

Since the scope of trade dress protection is unclear until it is actually litigated, many businesspeople have begun to register their businesses' trade dress. This is accomplished by registering the distinctive "look and feel," as discussed in chapter 11. By doing this, the proprietor gains added protection under the Lanham Act and body of law known as trade dress.

Individuals can also have distinctive styles. For example, when an advertiser hired one of Bette Midler's backup singers to replicate Ms. Midler's distinctive vocal rendition of a song for a commercial, Ms. Midler sued and recovered for the knockoff. It was held that the intentional copying of the singer's famous, distinctive style and voice was a form of infringement and actionable. When, however, a manufacturer hired a group that looked and sounded like the group known as The Fat Boys, the federal court in New York held the manufacturer liable only for violating the celebrities' publicity rights. The court refused to impose liability for the unauthorized use of The Fat Boys's sound since the New York publicity statute extends protection merely to one's "name, portrait or picture" and not to one's sound. The *Midler* case relied on the California statute that, among other things, protects a celebrity's voice.

Conclusion

While preparing an advertising program, it is essential for you to take care not to violate the rights of other businesses or individuals. Care should be taken to work with an attorney skilled in advertising law in order to be assured of having an effective program that will enable you to sell your product or service without exposing your business to potential liability. A poorly drafted advertising program is likely to be more harmful than none at all.

15

Cyberspace

It has become extremely popular for individuals and businesses to establish a presence on the World Wide Web. Elaborate home pages have been appearing with regularity for not only large multinational corporations but also for smaller companies. In fact, many small businesses have begun to construct Web sites, and the trend is growing. While there are no decisive studies on the extent of commerce that actually occurs on the Web, there is good indication that marketing on and surfing the Web has and will continue to become more commonplace. A study by the U.S. Commerce Department found that traffic on the Internet doubles every hundred days. The department predicted that electronic commerce will grow to $300 billion per year by 2002.

According to Meta Consulting Group, 80 percent of the businesses it surveyed in 1997 realized a positive return on their Web investments. Of the companies surveyed, there appeared to be no correlation between company size and Web site profitability. The businesses that did experience economic rewards averaged 38 percent return on their investments. Retail sales on the Web are thus far not common, however, according to America's Research Group in 1997, commercial activity in cyberspace is on the rise, albeit slowly.

America's Research Group survey also found that about 60 percent of U.S. households still do not own a computer, and about 85 percent of those that do, do not have a modem. Many home computers are not even powerful enough to surf the Web. The survey found that only 5 percent of the population is interested in using the Internet as a retail outlet, and more than half the consumers who have purchased something online say that they are not sure they will make any more purchases via the Web.

The use of Web sites for commercial activities is continuously expanding, however. At least one Internet advertising network, Double Click, is promoting an advertising program that will be result oriented. It has announced that it will charge only for successful results. Advertisers will only have to pay for the sales activity they actually capture on the Web.

Web sites have also been created for bill paying, securities sales, and airline bookings. In fact, the only limitations in cyberspace are the imaginations of users and the capacity of their equipment.

When the Social Security Administration and several private companies began putting financial data on the Web, problems arose. Despite the attempt to restrict access to this very sensitive information, individuals felt compromised. As a result of the widespread public dissatisfaction with the availability of so much personal information, the Social Security Administration closed its personal data site, and many others involved also agreed to voluntarily cease making available sensitive personal data. Some other companies have decided that financial information and other related personal data, such as magazine subscriptions and shopping habits, will not be disclosed on their Web sites. Unfortunately, not all businesses involved in information dissemination are cooperating, and since the arrangement is voluntary, there is no enforcement mechanism. The Internet will, therefore, continue to be a source of personal information for those who aggressively search for it.

Technology allows even the smallest business to create elaborate interactive sites that attract a good deal of positive attention. Theories abound on what makes a Web site appealing. For some, interactive graphics are the key; others feel it is important to provide browsers with something of value to take with them, such as information or the opportunity to obtain souvenirs of the visit. Some music publishers provide samples of the music they handle, while visual artists may encourage visitors to download images displayed on their sites.

Intellectual Property Protection

The World Wide Web's popularity has raised significant questions regarding the extent of legal and intellectual property protection in cyberspace. One of the earliest cases involved the Church of Scientology and raised the question of whether U.S. copyright laws and state trade secret laws are enforceable in cyberspace. In that case, a former church member was sued for posting copyrighted material on the World Wide Web that he had received in confidence.

The court held that these traditional forms of intellectual property protection were indeed applicable in cyberspace. In addition, it was held that the Internet access provider could also be exposed to liability for merely permitting the infringing material to appear on the Web. As elsewhere, one who facilitates or aids in the commission of an infringing act may be liable as a contributory infringer. Congress later changed this situation for Internet access providers who do not edit the content of the material posted.

The Church of Scientology also claimed that the wrongdoers misappropriated the church's trade secrets. It was alleged that the information posted on the Web by the former church member was confidential and protected under trade secret laws. The court rejected this argument, pointing out that once information is posted in cyberspace, it is no longer secret. As a result, anyone who downloads that information would not be guilty of trade secret misappropriation.

Certainly, if a protected trade secret is posted on a Web site in violation of an agreement or in breach of one's duty to the owner of the protected information, then the act of posting would be wrongful and the perpetrator would likely be liable for the improper activity. Cyberspace may be a new medium, but it is still a vehicle of communication and dissemination analogous to broadcasting on TV or publishing in a magazine.

Characterization of Web site names has also presented some vexing problems. It is unclear whether a domain name is merely an address used for the purpose of locating the site or whether that name may be characterized as a trademark. In addition, the problem is compounded by the fact that while there is only one World Wide Web, each trademark is distinguished by the classification of goods or services it covers. There are thirty-four international classes of goods and eight international classes of services. When, for example, the American Bar Association, commonly referred to as the ABA, wishes to register its acronym as its domain name, will it be able to displace the American Booksellers Association—also commonly known as the ABA?

Domain names have traditionally been registered with Network Solutions, though a nonprofit company called the American Registry for Internet Numbers has agreed to take over this service. Generally, domain names are registered on a first-come, first-served basis. A procedure has been adopted for the purpose of resolving conflicts if one of the parties has its trademark-cum-domain-name registered with the U.S. Patent and Trademark Office.

For example, when someone desires to register a domain name that is already in use by another, he or she must send a letter to the user of the domain name (the registrant) requesting that the name instead be assigned to him- or herself. If the registrant denies the request and the requester does, in fact, have a registered trademark in the requested name, a copy of the request letter should then be sent to the American Registry for Internet Numbers. Then, unless the registered party files suit for the purpose of obtaining a declaratory judgment establishing its prior right to the registered domain name, the site will be assigned to the trademark owner. In other words, the trademark owner may supplant the domain name registrant's right to that domain name if the registrant does not dispute the situation.

Note that this remedy is available only to owners of *registered* trademarks. If the party requesting the assignment has not yet registered the trademark, then the only way to obtain an assignment of a registered domain name is to file suit for trademark infringement and assignment of the domain name registration. This underscores the value of having a registered trademark.

Under some circumstances, using your business name as a domain name may be considered adequate for purposes of trademark registration. A number of cases have dealt with trademark issues in cyberspace. In those cases, the applicability of federal trademark law and the question as to which jurisdiction was proper for purposes of litigating the wrongdoing were considered. While the issues have not been definitively resolved, the trend appears to be in favor of extending trademark laws to cyberspace and holding infringers liable wherever their infringing activity can be accessed.

In one recent case, an enterprising individual residing in Illinois decided to register a number of popular business names as Web site domain names. When the business owners who had previously registered those names as trademarks attempted to obtain their company names as domain names, they were told that they were too late. The entrepreneuring registrant then offered to sell these companies the domain names for their own registered trademarks. The companies filed suit in California, alleging that the appropriation of the protected trademarks as domain names by one who lacks authority from the trademark owner is an infringement. The court agreed and suggested that this outrageous conduct would result in liability.

Moreover, the defendant in this case objected to being sued in California, stating that he was located in another state and that all his activity actually occurred within his home state. The California court made it clear that since the infringing site could be accessed in California, and since the infringer was trying to "extort" money for sale of the marks from California, the case could be properly brought there.

At least one case appears to have taken a different stance regarding jurisdiction. In that situation, a European restaurant bearing the same name as a restaurant in the United States established a Web site. The American company sued, alleging trademark infringement, and the court held that it was unlikely that the European restaurant would cause the kind of market confusion necessary to establish trademark infringement by advertising on the Web and having those advertisements viewed in the United States. Once again, though, this is consistent with intellectual property law in general in that it would appear that, even in cyberspace, it will be necessary to establish a "likelihood of confusion" and that the infringer somehow appropriates business from the owner of the protected trademark before liability will be imposed.

A number of other issues have generated Web-based litigation. When Total News, Inc., decided to provide Web surfers the ability to compare data from several news sources, such as *The Washington Post* and CNN, problems arose. The other services filed suit, complaining that the visual presentation of their material was "framed" within the host's name and that their protected material was, thereby, being retransmitted without their permission. The case was settled before trial with Total News agreeing to refrain from "framing" the protected material, and the plaintiffs agreed to grant Total News licenses to link directly to their sites. This case was settled before trial and not decided by a court. The question of the legality of "linking," where one may jump from one site to another by simply clicking on an identifying icon or phrase, was raised but not unresolved.

Internet Advertising

One of the most important distinctions of advertising on the Internet is the way cyberspace advertising reaches consumers. Ads in traditional advertising forums, such as magazines, newspapers, radio, and television, are intended to affect conduct in the future. It is hoped that the consumer will respond to a survey or purchase the product next time he or she goes shopping, or a radio or television advertisement may ask a consumer to actively contact a fulfillment center by phoning in an order. Internet shoppers, on the other hand, can instantaneously make a purchase.

Cyberspace may ultimately become a significant marketplace, but as of this writing, less than 2 percent of total advertising revenue is collected via the Internet. According to Elizabeth Wilkerson, senior counsel for Netscape Communications, advertising for print, radio, and television has now topped $175 billion dollars. Internet advertising revenue, however, was only $343.9 million during the first six months of 1997.

Laws adopted for purposes of preventing deceptive advertising do apply in cyberspace. The Federal Trade Commission (FTC) periodically conducts Internet surf days in conjunction with state attorneys general. The FTC requires certain disclosures in connection with certain forms of advertising, but these disclosures are easily lost in cyberspace. A disclosure can be by-passed when hyperlinking from one site to another and required legends can be buried in text that users may just scroll through. In contrast, when a disclosure appears in a more traditional advertisement, the viewer sees the entire composite—and required disclosures are unlikely to be bypassed.

According to the FTC, it is a good idea to require Web site visitors to click through required disclosures whenever an advertising site is visited. However, thus far, this policy has only resulted in the FTC announcing that it will sue a Web site designer if that designer knows or should have known that the site he or she created violates the law. Users have not been pressed into having to read disclosures if they do not want to.

Some intellectual property practitioners suggest that an attorney who has expertise in working with Web sites be requested to conduct a so-called internet traffic and Web-content audit. This would include evaluating whether the appropriate permissions to display material have been obtained. For example, if copyrighted material is to be used, has the copyright owner granted permission for the work to be displayed on the Web? If testimonials are to be displayed, then it is important to get written permission from the individual providing the testimonial.

Internet advertisers need to also determine whether their existing liability insurance covers their activity in cyberspace. Will your business be protected if your Web site crashes?

Since Web advertisements are, by definition, worldwide, it is meaningful to determine whether your site will subject you to liability elsewhere. As noted earlier in chapter 14, comparative advertising is generally permissible and fairly common in the United States; yet, other countries, such as Germany, are far more restrictive in what they permit in a comparative advertising ad.

Obscenity

An industry that has been extremely active in cyberspace is adult entertainment. Such sites have proliferated with extraordinary rapidity. Sites include everything from static two-dimensional images and printed matter to interactive real-time "cybersex." While some attempt has been made to restrict access to adults only, it has not been wholly successful. As a result, the U.S. Congress enacted the Communications Decency Act and many states followed this lead. This legislation was aimed at, among other things, preventing children from gaining access to sexually explicit material. Adult Web site owners immediately filed challenges to the legislation, however, and in June 1997, the U.S. Supreme Court, in *Reno v. ACLU,* unanimously declared some of the provisions of the Communications Decency Act to be unconstitutional. Justice John Paul Stevens, writing for the court, said,

> It is true that we have repeatedly recognized the governmental interest in protecting children from harmful materials. But that interest does not justify an unnecessarily broad suppression of speech addressed to adults. The government may not reduce the adult population . . . to . . . only what is fit for children. (*San Jose Mercury News*, June 26, 1997)

Several state courts declared similar state legislation to be unconstitutional since a state cannot restrict Web communication that is likely to be transmitted across state lines. Material that is transmitted on the Web is intended for communication throughout all of cyberspace. In fact, it is often impossible to determine the physical location of a Web site server. The extent of litigation that has resulted from activity on the World Wide Web suggests that care must be taken when establishing your presence in cyberspace. This new dimension gives rise to increased, and often desired, exposure, but the result can be devastating for a small business.

Even the simple act of advertising a product for retail sales could have serious consequences if you are not careful. For instance, if you market or sell a copyrighted item and even if you have obtained permission to advertise this item for sale, you may still not have the right to scan an image of that item into your computer and put it on your Web site. It may be necessary for you to obtain permission to replicate the work in two dimensions before engaging in cyberspace promotional activities.

Downloading and reusing material from other Web sites may also expose a business to liability. *Playboy* magazine has announced that it is developing an invisible electronic "watermark" to place on the images it posts on its Web site in order to discourage anyone from attempting to capture and reuse those images without permission. The company is also going to use a device to police cyberspace in order to locate any of its marked images.

Similarly, you have to recognize the fact that the Web is worldwide and that your material may find its way into jurisdictions and geographical regions that do not have copyright treaty relations with the United States. In this event, you may find that you have lost control of your protected work.

While the World Intellectual Property Organization (WIPO) has expanded the extent of protection available for intellectual property with the WIPO Treaty of 1996 and the SIPO Performances and Phonograms Treaty, not all countries have implemented these treaties. As of the date of this writing, approximately one hundred countries belong to WIPO, yet few have ratified these treaties to expand protection for sound recordings, motion pictures, computer software, and other digitally transmitted literary works. Even when the treaties are in force, there is still some risk since the treaties are limited in scope. Additionally, not all countries can be expected to participate and enact these treaties without reservation. Some countries will certainly remain on the U.S. watchlist since they continue to disregard their current treaty obligations, and there is no reason to believe these countries will adopt the new WIPO treaties.

Server Protection

Web sites may serve as windows to your company's computer system. If, for example, your business hosts its site on its own server that is networked with your other business computers, hackers may gain access to your entire system. There are some safeguards that should be taken in order to prevent improper access and protect your business's valuable trade secrets.

Information you deem to be confidential and sensitive should be encrypted. That is, it should only be available through use of special software. Similarly, your system should always be protected by a password, and that "word" should not be obvious or simple. More sophisticated systems will use "firewalls," which are electronic blocks preventing access to all but those who have the proper key. Many businesses have been created for the purpose of developing and installing computer security devices. You should consult with an expert when designing your Web site in order to take advantage of the latest technology.

The popularity of the World Wide Web has been paralleled by the expanded use of e-mail. Communications within the business are commonplace and efficient. Internal, paperless transmissions of important messages throughout an office or plant help facilitate the day-to-day operations in many businesses. Because of the widespread use of internal e-mail, business handbooks and policy statements should deal with the proper use of e-mail. For instance, it has been held that repeated transmission of sexually or racially explicit e-mail messages by one employee to another may be deemed harassment, and, if not controlled by the employer, may render the employer liable as well.

The external use of email is also quite common, enabling users to transmit complex documents worldwide in a format in which the recipient may edit the document as well as simply review it. Here, too, security is an issue to consider. If you are communicating with your attorney or doctor, is that transmission safe from uninvited inquisitors? Once again, there are vehicles available for security, such as encryption.

Internet e-mail is often abused. It has been held that persistent transmission of undesired electronic junk mail, commonly called "spam," continued after a request to stop is an actionable wrong. Regrettably, the advertisements and other uninvited literature that tends to clutter the traditional or "snailmail" mailbox has now found its way into the e-mail system.

By proceeding with good judgment and consulting with experienced intellectual property lawyers who have been involved with new technology, you can remain on the cutting edge of cyberspace.

For more information, you may wish to visit my firm's Web site at *www. artistic-law.com*

16

Warranty and Consumer Protection Laws

You may be warranting certain attributes of your business's products whether you realize it or not. The rules that govern warranties have been embodied in the Uniform Commercial Code, some form of which, as previously noted, has been adopted in all states and in most of the U.S. territories.

A warranty is, in essence, a guarantee that an item will be of a certain quality or have particular attributes. Giving a warranty involves certain obligations, so you should be aware of what those obligations are. Any statement of fact or promise that describes the characteristics of an item will create an *express warranty*. In general, you do not need to use the words *warranty* or *guarantee* to create an express warranty. However, the more explicit your statement, the more likely it is that you, perhaps unwittingly, have given an express warranty.

Elements of an Express Warranty

In order to determine whether statements are the type that will give rise to an express warranty—as opposed to mere expressions of opinion, which will not—the courts have developed a test. If the seller makes a statement to the buyer relating to goods about which the buyer is uninformed, that statement is probably an express warranty. On the other hand, if the seller merely expresses a judgment about something on which each party would be expected to have an opinion, no express warranty is given.

For example, if a manufacturer were to state that a ceramic bowl was oven-safe, this statement would likely be considered an express warranty since most buyers do not know much about pottery, and only the seller would know about this bowl in particular. In order to determine whether a statement will be considered an express warranty, a number of factors are relevant. A written statement, particularly if it is part of a contract or bill of sale, is more likely to be considered an express warranty than an oral statement. How much the seller qualifies the statement is also an indication of whether an express warranty is created.

Another way an express warranty can be created is by giving a description of the item that becomes part of the "basis of the bargain." The description does not need to be the sole inducement to purchase the goods in order for it to constitute a warranty. If a contract is involved, any statements must have been part of the contract negotiations, but the precise time a statement is made is irrelevant. The buyer could already have paid for an item and the seller could then make a statement that could be considered part of the basis of the bargain since, theoretically, the buyer could still decide to return the goods to the seller and get the money back. However, these postpurchase statements must be made within a reasonable period of time to be considered part of the bargain and they probably only apply to face-to-face dealings.

An additional problem presents itself if you sell your goods both through a catalogue or ads and in person. Catalogues or ads, and any statements made in them, could be considered part of the basis of the bargain for those making purchases in person, although buyers would probably have to prove that they relied on those statements in making the decision to purchase.

An express warranty can also be created by the use of samples or models. This type of warranty will arise if you sell from a catalogue or ship items from your stock after the buyer has viewed samples at a trade show. There is a distinction between a sample and a model. A sample is drawn from the actual goods that are the subject of the sale. Therefore, the sample describes the qualities of the goods being purchased unless the seller specifically states otherwise. For example, if you show a customer one placemat from a group of eight and the customer does not investigate the other seven, an express warranty is created that the remaining seven are of similar color, size, and composition as the one examined. On the other hand, a new model may not be drawn from the exact group of goods that are the subject of the sale. Therefore, a model is not quite as descriptive as a sample, but an express warranty can still be created.

Implied Warranties

In addition to express warranties, the Uniform Commercial Code imposes a number of *implied warranties* because such warranties are presumed to be part of the sales transaction. One of these, the implied warranty of merchantability, applies whenever the seller is a merchant. *Merchants* are defined as people who deal with goods of the kind involved in the sale or who, by their occupation, hold themselves out as having particular knowledge or skill. Merchants can also be those to whom this knowledge or skill can be attributed because they are acting as agents or intermediaries for a merchant.

Various tests for merchantability have been developed, including the following:

1. Does the item pass without objection in the trade under the description given in the contract between the buyer and seller?
2. Is the item at least fit for the ordinary purposes for which such goods are used?
3. Is the item adequately contained, packaged, and labeled as the contract or usage of trade may require?
4. Is the item of average quality based on the description given?
5. Does the item run within the variations permitted by the agreement between the buyer and seller? Are the items of a consistent kind, quality, and quantity within each unit and among units?
6. Does the item conform to any promises made on its container or label?

To be merchantable, an item need not be perfect. *Trade usage*, that is, the norms of a particular trade, will also establish the particular qualities that will be acceptable for items produced by members of that trade. Generally, the higher an item is priced, the more justifiable is the buyer's expectation of high quality.

When a seller knows of a particular purpose for which the buyer is purchasing the goods and knows the buyer is relying on the seller's skill or judgment to choose something suitable, there is an implied warranty that the goods will fit such a purpose. The usual way this warranty is created is when the buyer asks the seller for assistance. For example, if an individual comes to you and requests assistance in choosing a bedspread for a baby's crib, an implied warranty is created. The implied warranty would probably include at least two specific attributes: (1) that the bedspread is not made out of any toxic materials so that the baby can safely put it in his or her mouth and (2) that it can be washed without running or shrinking, unless you specifically tell the buyer it must be dry-cleaned or hand-washed.

"A particular purpose" means a specific purpose for a specific buyer's use. Therefore, purchasing an item because it aesthetically pleases the buyer probably is not a particular purpose. It is an ordinary purpose. A particular purpose must be reasonably specific and explicit in order to assume that the seller has been informed of the buyer's purpose. In this regard, if the buyer is knowledgeable about what you sell, it is less likely that this implied warranty is created. The one exception to this warranty is when a buyer asks for a particular brand or a particular company's product. In that case, the buyer is not relying on the seller's skill and judgment, so no implied warranty is created.

A *warranty of title* is implied in every contract for sale of goods. It simply means that the seller has good title, or the right to sell the item, and that the seller is unaware of any outstanding lien against the item. The seller does not need to be a merchant, as defined above, and is not saved from liability by ignorance of a defect in the title. This warranty is based on the commonsense idea that a buyer should not have to defend ownership of goods against the claims of a third party.

The most modern of the implied warranties is the implied warranty against infringement. When an item is sold, the seller warrants that the item is not infringing any rights protected by patent, trademark, copyright, or trade dress. If it appears that the object was created in violation of a third person's intellectual property rights, this warranty is breached.

At one time, there may have been some technical legal defenses available to a defendant who, as a manufacturer, did not sell a defective item directly to an injured person. It now appears that the vast majority of states would permit a victim to sue the retailer, wholesaler, manufacturer, or component-part manufacturer for injuries sustained as a result of a defective product.

Disclaimers

What can you do if you do not want to give one or more of these express or implied warranties? You can use a disclaimer, but it must be given in certain specific ways.

To be safe, disclaimers should be in writing. When you have given an express warranty, it is difficult to disclaim it. It is considered unreasonable to give an express warranty and then turn around and disclaim it. Therefore, *an attempt to disclaim an express warranty will usually not be successful.* This includes any express warranties that may be set forth in a description of an item. Also, you cannot limit the time period within which the buyer must discover any disclaimers contained in the warranty.

A common problem results when a customer claims that oral warranties were made before the signing of a written contract. The seller may be shielded from this problem by a rule that sometimes prevents prior oral statements from being considered as part of the contract. However, there are exceptions that you should be aware of. If there is a written agreement and it is not the final agreement, the written agreement will not supersede prior oral express warranties. Also, if the oral terms are consistent with a written disclaimer, they will be considered binding if the writing was not intended as a complete and exclusive statement of the terms. These types of problems tend to arise most often when someone else sells your goods for you. If you often have a salesperson sell your goods, you would be wise to include a limitation of the salesperson's authority on any written receipt.

Implied warranties can also be disclaimed. To exclude or modify the implied warranty of merchantability, the word *merchantability* must be specifically mentioned and the disclaimer must be conspicuous. This warranty can be disclaimed orally. The implied warranty of fitness for a particular purpose, however, can be disclaimed only in writing. Meanwhile, the implied warranty of title can be disclaimed only by specific language or by circumstances which give the buyer reason to know that the seller does not have title or that the seller's title is subject to a third party's interest.

You are well advised to consult with an attorney to determine which warranties should be disclaimed and the best method of accomplishing this. The rules on disclaimers are quite technical and care must be taken in determining how much exposure you may have in a particular situation.

If you decide to give a written warranty or disclaim warranty protection in writing, you should be aware that there are federal regulations promulgated under the Magnuson-Moss Warranty Act to cover consumer products. According to the act, all of the following must be indicated in a written warranty:

- To whom the warranty is extended
- Exactly what parts of the product are covered
- What the warrantor will do in case of defect
- When the warranty begins and ends
- What the buyer has to do to get warranty coverage
- Any limitations on the duration of implied warranties (this is not allowed in some states)
- Any exclusions or limitations regarding relief

In the written warranty, you must also specify what you are promising regarding the material and workmanship and specify that the item is defect-free or will meet a specific level of performance. You must also clearly indicate whether the warranty is full or limited. Under a *full warranty*, the warrantor agrees to the following:

- To remedy the product within a reasonable period of time without charge if the product has a defect, malfunction, or fails to conform to the written warranty
- Not to impose a limitation on implied warranties
- Not to exclude or limit "consequential" damages unless this is clear on the face of the warranty

- To replace the item or refund the purchase price if the item is unsuccessfully repaired numerous times

If any one of the above qualifications is not met, you have given a *limited warranty*.

If you breach a warranty and the buyer is damaged by your failure to comply with the warranty obligations, the buyer may sue and you may be ordered to pay damages, court costs, and reasonable attorney's fees. Since this remedy exists, you should be careful to determine which warranties you are giving and learn how to disclaim them if you do not want to give them.

Consumer Protection Laws

Cooling-off Period for Field Sales

The federal government and many states have enacted legislation designed to give consumers the opportunity to change their minds and cancel an unwanted sale. The federal law generally applies to any sale, loan, or rental of consumer goods or services that has a purchase price of $25 or more. This only applies when the seller or the seller's representative personally solicits the sale and the buyer's agreement, or offer to purchase, is made at a place other than the seller's place of business. The seller's "place of business" is defined as the main or permanent branch office or local address of the seller.

These laws protect the consumer by offering a cooling-off period within which to notify the seller of intention to cancel the purchase. The consumer may receive a return of all money paid and rescind any contract signed without further obligation. In effect, the consumer is given a period of time, typically up to midnight of the third business day following the sale, during which to determine whether he or she really wants to go through with the transaction.

The seller's principal obligation under these regulations is to disclose to the potential consumer that such a cooling-off period exists and that it is the consumer's right to take advantage of that escape clause and cancel the sale if desired. The form and content of this disclosure requirement is spelled out in the federal regulations.

To comply with the statute, a seller must be prepared to furnish the buyer with a fully completed receipt or copy of any agreement pertaining to the sale at the time the sale is made or the agreement is signed. The receipt or agreement must be in the same language that was principally used in the oral sales presentation. For example, if the presentation was made in Spanish, the receipt or agreement must also be in Spanish. The receipt or agreement must also include the seller's name and address, time and date of sale, and a statement on the first page that contains the following language: "You, the buyer, may cancel this transaction at any time prior to midnight of the third business day after the date of this transaction. See the attached notice-of-cancellation form for an explanation of this right." The notice-of-cancellation form must detail the buyer's rights and obligations in the event the buyer chooses to cancel the sale.

In addition to the federal regulation, many states have enacted similar consumer protection statutes that provide for a cooling-off period and contain a similar disclosure requirement. It is strongly advised that if you engage in consumer sales other than from a permanently established business location, you confer with an attorney who can advise you of the legal requirements in your particular state.

Mail-Order Sales

A popular method of selling is through mail-order services or catalogue sales. Here, too, the federal government has established certain guidelines aimed at protecting the consuming public. When a seller solicits a sale through the mail or through a mail-order catalogue, the seller must reasonably expect to be able to ship any ordered merchandise to the buyer within the time stated in the solicitation. If no time period is stated, the merchandise must be shipped within thirty days after receiving a properly completed order. If the seller is unable to ship the merchandise within the specified time limit, the seller must offer the buyer the option either of consenting to a delay in shipping or of canceling the order and receiving a prompt refund. The seller is also required to inform the buyer of any anticipated delays in shipping and to explain why the shipping deadline cannot be met.

Legal Advice Regarding Risks

You should consult with a business lawyer to evaluate the extent of exposure that may be expected as a result of the numerous warranties and consumer protection laws that apply to sales. Where appropriate, warranty disclaimers and notices of right of cancellation, as well as limitations of liability, can be used to reduce your exposure, but skilled drafting is necessary for effective protection. In addition, product liability insurance (see the next chapter) may be procured as a means of insulating yourself from extensive liability.

17

Product Liability

In November of 1978, a California jury awarded the victim of an automobile accident $120 million after his defectively designed Ford Pinto caught fire and exploded, inflicting serious personal injury. The size of this judgment against the Ford Motor Company staggered the nation.

Unless you happen to own a Pinto, you may ask, What does this have to do with me? The answer is that if you regularly sell a product, you might find yourself in court being sued by one of your customers for an injury if the customer claims that something you created was defective. The same laws that apply to the sale of a car by Ford apply to a sale by you. In one sense, it seems quite logical and fair that the laws apply equally to all regardless of size. When we take a closer look at the law, however, we see that it was not designed with the small business in mind.

History of Liability Law

To understand the present state of liability law, it might be useful to briefly examine its roots. In 1804, a craftsman named Seixas went to a warehouse to buy some brazilletto wood. I have never run across any myself, but the learned judge who wrote the legal opinion assured posterity that it was of considerable value. Woods, the warehouse man, sold Seixas some peachum wood, which is virtually worthless, instead. Neither party apparently knew the difference between brazilletto and peachum.

When Seixas discovered the error, he tried to return the worthless wood in exchange for either brazilletto or his money. The warehouse man refused because he had already given the money to the original owner of the wood. Seixas sued Woods and lost. Seixas lost, even though Woods had written *brazilletto* on the invoice, because the wood had never been warranted as such. Besides, the seller, Woods, did not know any more about different kinds of wood than the buyer, Seixas, did.

The result of this case can be amply summed up in the Latin maxim *caveat emptor*: let the buyer beware. This maxim was repeated time and again in both English and American cases until comparatively recent times. But now the pendulum has swung the other way and the rule has become *caveat vendor*: let the seller beware. The change came about gradually.

One of the harshest rules of early product liability cases was that people injured by defective products could not sue the manufacturers unless they purchased directly from them. This technical requirement was carried down the distribution lines so that only individuals who dealt directly with each other had rights against each other, and consumers could not sue anyone but the retailers with whom they had traded.

This doctrine was recognized as harsh and formalistic; thus, it was not followed in a number of situations. For example, a seller, regardless of position in the chain of distribution, could be sued if negligent and if the product was "inherently dangerous." The courts struggled for some time over just what was and what was not inherently dangerous.

At least one early case said a car was not inherently dangerous. Justice Benjamin Cardozo, in a landmark decision, disagreed. To him, a product was inherently dangerous if injury to the owner was predictable in cases where the item was defective. Almost anything can be injurious if defective, and that decision holds today. Where once a car was not deemed inherently dangerous, now negligence suits have been brought for such seemingly innocuous items as a toy top, rubber boots, and a lounge chair.

Cardozo made several other important pronouncements in the field of product liability. For example, he stated that a manufacturer could be liable for defects in component parts made by another manufacturer if the assembler did not inspect them. This shift of the burden of responsibility from the buyer to the seller is a natural response to several factors. First, as products became increasingly more complex, it was no longer true that the buyer and seller were equally knowledgeable or uninformed. Second, it was felt that businesses were large enough to bear the immediate losses and, ultimately, could spread the risk over a broad number of consumers. Since the majority of the products on today's market are mass-produced by large manufacturers, the rule reflects present economic reality.

Unfortunately, this is not the economic reality of the small business; yet, it too must learn to cope with these laws in a climate of litigious consumers and generous juries. It is better to learn about these problems while you can still protect yourself rather than when it is too late.

Product Liability

In every product liability case, the plaintiff must prove that:
1. Injury occurred to the plaintiff
2. The injury was caused by some defect in the product
3. The defect was present in the product when the defendant had control over it

Once people are in possession of your product, you will not be able to stop them from injuring themselves. You can control this third element, however, by making sure that any item that leaves your control does not contain a defect.

There are two kinds of defects: *mechanical defects*, such as loose screws and faulty component parts, and *design defects*, such as instability, flammability, toxicity, and tendency to shatter.

Mechanical Defects

Under the current rule of "strict liability" followed by a majority of the states, you can be held liable even for defects that could not have been discovered or prevented by human skill, knowledge, or foresight. Your only protection is insurance.

Many defects *are* detectable before an accident occurs if the right tests are made. Following Cardozo's lead, the courts have held that manufacturers have a duty to inspect and test their goods. Failure to adequately test has been held reason enough to impose large awards of punitive damages on top of the actual damages awarded.

How much testing is adequate? Sophisticated testing might prove to be too expensive for the small business. My advice is to design the best test you can for whatever you make, even if it is only a good tug here and there. Most importantly, keep a record of it. This may serve to prove that you attempted to fulfill your duty to test the product. While this precaution might not protect you from product liability, it may result in reducing, if not eliminating, punitive-damage awards against you.

It is rare for an injured plaintiff to be able to prove that a defect was present when a product was purchased. The plaintiff frequently must rely on inferences drawn from the accident itself. If the jury is convinced that there is better than a fifty-fifty chance that the defect was there when the product was bought, the plaintiff will probably win. However, if you come into court with a record of tests on your product, the odds might shift in your favor.

Besides keeping records of your tests, you should also keep records of your purchases of materials and devise some method of identifying the components in your product. That way, if you are sued for a defect in a component part, you can pass the liability on to the party really at fault. For example, if a stained-glass window collapses because the camming is inferior, you might be able to pass your liability on to the manufacturer of the defective cam.

Design Defects

The category of design defects can be further subdivided into those that violate a statute and those that do not. A 1959 case contains a good example of how far a court might go in defining a design defect. A rather obese woman entered a store and sat in a chair of contemporary design that the store had for sale. The back of the chair curved elegantly into the seat, which, in turn, curved down and around to form the base of the chair. It was along these serpentine curves that the overweight customer slid onto the floor. The injury to her pride was aggravated by an injury to her spine. The court held that the shape of the chair was defective and awarded her $25,000 in damages.

In defective-design cases, the courts have usually adhered to a commonsense criterion. If the product conformed to the *state of the art* when it was made, it will usually not be held defective. The state of the art is *not* the same as industrywide standards. Industrywide standards may be introduced in evidence, but it cannot be assumed that these assure due care. This is because the law will not allow an industry to adopt sloppy practices in order to save money or time when better, more protective methods are available. The state of the art, on the other hand, determines the norm for an industry based on how far technology in the relevant field has advanced.

In addition, a design may be defective if it does not meet the standards set forth in a statute. No product should be sold for consumer use before a check has been made to see whether it is covered by a consumer protection law. A violation of these laws may carry criminal sanctions. In some jurisdictions, consumers injured by a product have proven their case merely by proving that a statute was violated in the production or sale of the product. The manufacturer would then have the burden of establishing that the injury was not the result of the statutory violation, which would be almost impossible in cases where the law had been enacted to prevent the very type of injury alleged.

Federal Laws

Not only is there state legislation pertaining to liability, there are at least three federal laws that directly affect the manufacturer. The first of these is a group of acts: the Hazardous Substance Labeling Act, as amended by the Child Protection Act of 1966 and the Child Protection and Toy Safety Act of 1969. These laws were passed in response to the staggering number of injuries and poisonings that occur each year to children under the age of fifteen. They empower the Federal Trade Commission to name any potentially dangerous material a *hazardous substance*. Such substances may not be used in *any product* that might give a child access to the hazardous substance. That is, no amount of use or abuse by a child should make the product unsafe. Presently banned under this act are jaquirty beans used in necklaces, jewelry, and dolls' eyes. For a list of other hazardous substances, you should consult your local office of the FTC. Its Web site address is: *www. ftc.gov/*.

The second statute is the Flammable Fabrics Act. This statute empowers the FTC to establish appropriate standards of flammability for the fabrics used in clothing and household products, including children's toys.

Finally, there is the Consumer Product Safety Act, a statute that empowers the FTC to regulate the composition, content, and design of any consumer product. The FTC has promulgated regulations for the use of architectural glass in doors, windows, and walls and has banned the use of surface-coating materials (paints) containing lead. This is a dynamic area and all manufacturers should check with the FTC to determine whether the materials used in their products are subject to regulation.

Under the current law of product liability, a seller held liable for a defective product may, in turn, seek reimbursement from the manufacturer for the amount paid in damages. This may involve another expensive lawsuit, and if the manufacturer is broke, the seller is out of luck. There are two things that a seller might do for protection. First, incorporate or use another business form that offers limited liability. This business method is complex and is discussed in detail in chapter 1. The second method of self-protection is to obtain insurance.

Liability Insurance

In general, the cost of liability insurance is affordable for the small business: $100,000 liability insurance for a person doing only $10,000 of business a year may cost as little as $100 annually, although rates will vary from region to region. You should consult your insurance broker or agent to ascertain the rates in your particular area. Many trade associations provide product liability insurance to their members for reasonable prices. You should determine whether you can obtain this form of insurance from professional trade or business associates you are involved with. You must then evaluate this cost against the risk of a lawsuit. Many product liability suits are settled for, or are litigated to a judgment of, over $100,000. You can deduct the cost of this kind of insurance as a business expense for tax purposes. Given these factors, if there is any reasonable expectation that a purchaser of your product could sustain personal injury from it, you should seriously consider obtaining product liability insurance.

Clearly, the area of product liability has evolved to a point where manufacturers are being held liable for injuries caused by their defective products. The doctrines appear to have evolved with an eye to the large manufacturer of a mass-produced item, but the rules are applied with the same vigor to the small manufacturer. Since a single lawsuit could ruin a small business, it is important to be aware of the potential risks involved and to take the necessary precautions.

18 Business Insurance

Today's insurance business originated sometime in the late seventeenth century in a London coffeehouse called Lloyd's. Lloyd's was a popular gathering place for seamen and merchants engaged in foreign trade. As Shakespeare pointed out in *The Merchant of Venice*, great profit can come from a successful sea voyage, but financial disaster can follow just as surely from a loss of ships at sea. From past experience, these merchants knew that despite their greatest precautions, such disaster could strike any one of them.

Through their dealings with the Italians, the merchants had become familiar with the notion of insurance, but there was no organized insurance company in England at that time. When these merchants were together at Lloyd's, it became a custom to arrange for mutual insurance contracts. The method employed was for a ship's owner, before the ship embarked, to pass around a slip of paper that described the ship, its captain and crew, its destination, and the nature of the cargo. Those merchants who wished to be insurers of that particular ship would initial this slip and indicate the extent to which they could be held liable. This slip was circulated until the entire value of the ship and cargo was covered. This method of creating insurance contracts was called "underwriting."

Today, the term *underwriting* is used to describe the formation of any insurance contract, regardless of the means employed to consummate it. Lloyd's of London still uses a method similar to that which originated in the coffeehouse, but most other insurance companies assume the payment of losses out of their own financial holdings.

The risks covered by insurance, too, have changed. The original Lloyd's dealt in maritime insurance only. Now, almost anything can be insured—from a pianist's hands to a Concorde jet.

Why Insurance for the Small Business?

Although your business may not be as perilous as that of a seventeenth-century merchant, it is not altogether free of risks. Let me mention just a few of those risks.

Recent crime statistics show that even in rural areas you may become the victim of burglary. Various methods may be employed to protect against burglary, but none is perfect.

The forces of nature—fire, flood, earthquake—are undiscriminating in their targets. If you operate out of your home, you may already have homeowner's insurance against these, but you may find that your insurance is inadequate to cover your supplies and inventory. In fact, your homeowner's insurance may not cover these at all, as will be discussed later in this chapter.

A sale of your products subjects you to virtually unlimited liability to anyone who may be injured by one of them, no matter how careful you may have been in creating them. The potential magnitude of what this could cost you makes even the slightest chance of its occurrence a significant risk.

Loss of earnings through sickness or accident is a risk common to all small businesses. Some businesses that rely on a small number of partners for essential work may suffer a loss of earnings due to a loss of partners through sickness or accident. This risk is far too often overlooked.

Many risks can be insured against through any number of insurance companies. It should be noted, though, that there are some things against which you *cannot* insure. Insurance has a certain air of gambling to it. You put down some money and if a certain event occurs, you get back many times more. If it does not occur, you get back nothing. That is where the similarity ends.

Public policy will not permit you to insure something unless you have what is called an *insurable interest*. To have an insurable interest, you must have a property right, a contract right, or a potential liability that would result in a real loss to you if a given event occurs. The reason behind this is simply to minimize the temptation to cause the calamity against which you are insured. History contains too many gruesome stories of desperate or crazy people obtaining insurance on a neighbor's barn or even a neighbor's child. Because of issues like these, most kinds of insurance, particularly liability insurance, do not cover injuries that are intentionally caused by the policyholder.

Of course, the requirement of an insurable interest has never stopped anyone from hastening that interest's demise or destruction. Recently, two businessmen were overheard at a party. One told the other that he had recovered one million dollars in fire insurance that year. The other businessman said he recovered *two* million for loss caused by a windstorm. The first, with greed in his eyes, asked, "How do you start a windstorm?"

The Basics of Insurance Law

Before analyzing the mechanics of choosing whether or not to insure a particular risk, I will briefly outline the law of insurance. All insurance is based on a contract between the insurer and the insured whereby the insurer assumes a specified risk for a fee called a *premium*. The insurance contract must contain at least all of the following:

1. A definition of whatever is being insured (the subject matter)
2. The nature of the risks insured against
3. The maximum possible recovery
4. The duration of the insurance
5. The due date and amount of the premiums

When the amount of recovery has been predetermined in the insurance contract, it is called a *valued* policy. An *unvalued* or *open* insurance policy covers the full value of property up to a specified policy limit. I will be discussing the advantages and disadvantages of each in this chapter.

The insurance contract does more than merely shift the risk from the insured to the insurance company. The insurance industry is regulated by state law so as to spread the risk among those subject to that same risk. The risk-spreading is accomplished by defining the method used for determining the amount of the premium to be paid by the insured. First, the insurance company obtains data on the actual loss sustained by a defined class within a given period of time. State law regulates just how the company may define the class. An insurance company may not, for example, separate white homeowners and nonwhite homeowners into different classes, but it may separate drivers with many accidents from drivers with few.

Next, the company divides the risk equally among the members of the class. Then the company adds a fee for administrative costs and profits. This amount is regulated from state to state. Finally, the premium is set for each individual in proportion to the likelihood that a loss will occur.

Besides the method of determining premiums, state insurance laws usually specify the training necessary for agents and brokers, the amount of commission payable to them, and the kind of investments the insurance company may make with the premiums.

The very documents that a company uses to make insurance contracts are regulated from state to state. Sometimes the state requires a standard form from which the company may not deviate, especially for fire insurance. A growing number of states require that "plain English" be used in all forms. Plain English is measured in reference to the average number of syllables per word and the average number of words per sentence. Because of a federal ruling that all insurance contracts are, per se, fraudulent if they exceed certain maximum averages, the insurance companies are forced to write contracts that an average person can understand. Nevertheless, only insomniacs read most insurance forms.

Expectations versus Reality

One frequent result of the gobbledygook used in most insurance contracts is that the signed contract may differ in some respect from what the agent may have led the insured person to expect. If you can prove that an agent actually lied, then the agent will be personally liable to you for the amount of promised coverage. In addition, the insurance company itself may be liable for the wrongful acts of its agents.

Most often, the agent will not lie but will accidentally neglect to inform the insured of some detail. For instance, if you want insurance for transporting your products, the agent may sell you a policy that covers transport only in public carriers—when you intended to rent a truck and transport the products yourself. In most states, the courts hold that it is the duty of the insured to read the policy before signing. In the above example, if you neglect to read the clause that limits coverage to a public carrier, you would be out of luck.

In other, more progressive states, this doctrine has been considered too harsh. These states will allow an insured to challenge specific provisions in the signed contract to the extent they do not conform to reasonable expectations resulting from promises that the agent made. In the example above, it might be considered reasonable to expect that you would be insured when transporting your own goods. If the agent did not specifically call your attention to this limitation in the contract, odds are that you would have a good case for getting rid of it. In addition, it is common for the insured to receive the policy only after the premium is paid, or only after a specific request is made.

Other states follow a different approach for contract interpretation and attempt to ascertain the intention of the parties. The first step in interpreting an insurance policy is to examine the text and context of the policy as a whole. If, after that examination, two or more conflicting interpretations remain reasonable, the ambiguity is resolved against the insurer. A court in these states will assume that parties to an insurance contract do not create meaningless provisions and will favor the interpretation that lets all provisions have meaning.

Of course, I would not advise waiting for an agent to point out unexpected policy variations even in the most liberal state. You should read the contract with the agent. If it is unintelligible, ask the agent to list on a separate sheet all the important aspects before signing, and keep that sheet.

Reforming the Contract

After the insurance contract has been signed, its terms can be *reformed* (revised) only to comply with the original agreement from which the written contract may somehow have deviated.

Let's consider the case of a woman who inherited a pearl necklace. An appraiser, apparently hoping for a large fee, misled her and told her the pearls were genuine and, therefore, worth $60,000. Before having them shipped from the estate, she obtained insurance on them in the amount of $60,000, paying a premium of $2,450. In the description of the subject matter, it was stated that the pearls were genuine. The pearls were ruined after they arrived at the delivery terminal, but before she received them. She tried to collect the $60,000.

In the course of the investigation of the accident, it was discovered that the pearls were not natural but cultured, and were worth only $61.50. Of course, the insured could not collect $60,000 because no natural pearls were lost or damaged. The worst of it was that she could not collect even $61.50 because the policy did not cover cultured pearls. The court emphasized that for reformation of the contract to be granted, there must have been something either included or omitted contrary to the intention of both parties. In this case, neither party ever intended to include cultured pearls, so the court refused to make a contract for the parties covering cultured pearls.

You might think that in this case the insured would get back her premium because there were never any genuine pearls to insure. She argued this, but lost again. The court reasoned that had the pearls been lost in transit, instead of being later destroyed, the actual value of the pearls would never have come to light. Therefore, the insurance company had indeed assumed the risk of paying out $60,000 and was entitled to the premium.

Overinsuring and Underinsuring

This case does not mean that if an insured accidentally overvalues the goods, no insurance will be recovered. Had the pearls been natural, but worth only $20,000, she would have recovered $20,000. Note that overinsurance does not entitle one to a recovery beyond the actual value of the goods insured. This is because one does not have an insurable interest beyond the actual value of an item. To allow a recovery greater than the value of the goods would be no different than allowing people to gamble with insurance policies.

Since you can, at best, break even with insurance, you might think it would be profitable to underinsure your goods. You could gain by paying lower premiums and lose only in the event that the damage exceeds the policy maximum. This has been tried and failed.

Let us study a case where the insured stated the value of her unscheduled property as $9,950 and obtained insurance on that amount. *Unscheduled property* means an undetermined collection of goods—for example, all a person's clothes and furniture—which may change from time to time. In this case, a fire occurred causing at least $9,950 damage.

The insurance company investigated the claim and determined that the insured owned at least $36,500 in unscheduled property. The company refused to pay on grounds that the insured obtained the insurance fraudulently. The court agreed with the insurance company, stating that the intentional failure to communicate the full value of the unscheduled property rendered the entire contract void. Therefore, the insured could not even collect the policy maximum. All she could hope for, at best, would be to get her premiums back.

Although at first glance this decision may seem harsh, its ultimate fairness becomes apparent with a little analysis. The chance of losing $9,950 out of $36,500 is greater than the chance of losing $9,950 out of $9,950 simply because most accidents or thefts do not result in total losses.

Various tests are used by the courts to determine whether an omission or misstatement renders such a policy void. In almost all cases, the omission or misstatement must be intentional or obviously reckless, and it must be material to the contract. Materiality is typically measured with reference to the degree of importance that the insurance company ascribes to the omitted or misstated fact. If stating the fact correctly would have significantly affected the conditions or premiums that the company would demand, then the fact is likely material. In the above case, had the full value of the unscheduled property been stated, the insurer would either have demanded that the full value be insured, or that a higher premium be paid for the limited coverage. Thus, the misstatement was clearly material.

Unintentional Undervaluing

It should be noted that not all undervaluations will be material. Many insurance contracts do allow some undervaluation where it is unintentional. This provision is designed to protect the insured from inflation, which causes property to increase in replacement value before the policy's renewal date.

A so-called *coinsurance clause* generally provides that the insured may recover 100 percent of any loss up to the face value of the policy provided the property is insured for at least 80 percent of its full value. For example, if a house worth $100,000 was insured for $80,000 and suffered a $79,000 loss from a covered casualty, the insured would recover the full amount of the loss, or $79,000. If the property was only insured for $50,000, then a formula would be used to determine the amount of recovery. This formula requires you to establish a ratio between the amount of insurance coverage and the total value of the property and then multiply the resulting fraction by the loss to get the recovery.

This gives us $50,000 (insurance) divided by $100,000 (value of building) times $79,000 (loss) = $39,500 (recovery). This example points out the importance of carrying insurance on at least 80 percent of the value of your property. Considering inflation, it is wise to reexamine your coverage each year.

All insurance policies are limited to certain defined subject matter and to losses caused to that subject matter by certain defined risks. Once the risks are recognized, it is a simple matter to decide whether or not to insure against them. However, correctly defining the subject matter of insurance is tricky business. Mistakes here are not uncommon and can result in anyone finding themselves uninsured—like the woman with the pearl necklace.

Scheduling Property

The typical insurance policy will include various exclusions and exemptions. For example, most homeowner and auto-insurance policies cover personal property but exclude business property. If a manufacturer keeps certain products at home for personal enjoyment, are they personal or business property? The answer depends on whether the person ever sells or displays any of these goods. If any are sold or displayed, this may convert them all to business property.

In order to avoid the potentially tragic loss of such property, the manufacturer may schedule the pieces that are held for personal enjoyment. *Scheduling* is a form of inventorying where the insured submits a list and description of all pieces to be insured with an appraisal of their value. The insurer assumes the risk of loss of all scheduled works without concern as to whether or not they pertain to the business. Insurance on scheduled property is slightly more expensive than that on unscheduled property.

Many battles occur over the value of objects stolen, destroyed, or lost. In anticipation of such battles, you should maintain records of sales to establish the market price of goods and an inventory of all goods on hand. In the case of certain kinds of property (artwork, for example), the value must be determined by an expert in the field. However, this will not avoid all problems because the insurance company can always contest the scheduled value.

When and How to Insure

We now come to the most important issues: how to decide whether or not to insure and how to go about obtaining insurance.

Deciding Factors

Three factors should be weighed to determine whether or not to obtain insurance. First, you must set a value on that which is to be insured. Health is of the utmost value and should always be insured. Material goods are valued according to the cost of replacement. If you keep a large inventory of goods or if you own expensive equipment, it probably should be insured. The most elementary way to determine if the value is sufficiently high to necessitate insurance is to rely on the pain factor; if it would hurt to lose it, insure it.

Second, you must estimate the chances that a given calamity will occur. An insurance broker can tell you what risks are prevalent in your line of work or in your neighborhood. You should supplement this information with your personal knowledge. For example, you may know that your workshop is virtually fireproof or that only a massive flood would cause any real damage. Although these facts should be weighed in your decision, you should not be guilty of audaciously tempting fate. As the great tragedians have recounted, to scoff at disaster is to invite it. If the odds are truly slim, but some risk is still present, the premium will be correspondingly smaller in most cases.

The third factor is the cost of the insurance. Bear in mind that insurance purchased to cover your business is tax deductible. This means that if you pay tax at a 31 percent rate, Uncle Sam is theoretically paying for 31 percent of your premium.

Keeping the Cost Down

As already explained, the premiums charged by an insurance company are regulated by the government. Nonetheless, it still pays to shop around. Insurance companies can compete by offering different packages of insurance and by hiring competent agents to assist you in your choice.

If there are enough small-business owners in your area engaged in a similar business of similar size, it may be possible for you to form a co-op insurance fund. To do this, you must estimate the total losses your co-op would sustain in the course of a year. Each member then contributes a pro rata share. The money is put into a bank to collect interest. If a disaster occurs and the losses are greater than the fund, each member must contribute to make up the difference. If there is money left over, it can be used to lessen the following year's premiums. This method is cheaper than conventional insurance because it eliminates insurance agents' commissions and whatever you would have paid toward the profit earned by the insurance company. But before you form your co-op, you should contact an attorney to determine what regulations exist in your state.

People Who Work for You

There comes a time in the life of almost every small business when it is necessary to get help, be it brain or brawn. The help most commonly needed first is the bookkeeper or accountant who can handle taxes, billing, and the like. When things get a little hectic around the shop or office, you might then hire someone to help with the packing or running errands. If selling is not your greatest talent, you may engage the services of a salesperson or a manufacturer's representative. If this salesperson is really good, you will soon have to hire more employees to keep up with the demand.

Independent Contractors

Someone hired on a one-time or job-by-job basis is called an *independent contractor*. Although paid for their services by the hiring firm or individual, contractors remain their own bosses and may even employ others to actually do the work.

If you occasionally give products to a friend to sell on consignment, the friend is probably an independent contractor. If you hire a bookkeeper or accountant once or twice a year to go over your business records, that person, too, is an independent contractor. The fact that the person is independent and not your employee means that you do not have to pay social security, withhold income taxes, obtain a workers' compensation policy, or comply with the myriad rules imposed on employers.

More importantly, you are generally not liable for injuries to a third party resulting from the independent contractor's negligence or wrongful acts even while working for you. However, there are situations where, despite your innocence, an independent contractor can render you legally responsible for his or her wrongful acts. Such situations fall into the following three basic categories:

1. If an employer is careless in hiring an independent contractor, and a careful investigation would have disclosed facts to indicate that the contractor was not qualified, the employer may be liable when the independent contractor fails to properly perform the job.

2. If a job is so dangerous as to be characterized as "ultrahazardous" (a legal term), and is to be performed for the employer's benefit, then regardless of who performs the work, the employer will remain legally responsible for any injuries that occur during the performance of the work. A fireworks displayer, for example, cannot escape liability by having fuses lit or rockets aimed by independent contractors.

3. An employer may be required by law to perform certain tasks for the health and safety of the community.

These responsibilities are said to be nondelegable—that is, an employer cannot delegate them and, thus, escape liability for their improper performance. If, therefore, a nondelegable duty is performed by an independent contractor, the employer will remain responsible for any injury that results. A good example of a nondelegable duty is the law (common in many states) that homeowners are responsible for keeping their sidewalks free of dangerous obstacles. If a homeowner hires an independent contractor to fulfill this obligation by removing ice during the winter, the homeowner is still legally liable if someone is injured on the slippery sidewalk even if the accident resulted from the contractor's carelessness.

Employees

The second capacity in which someone can work for you is as an *employee*. This category includes anyone over whose work you exercise direct control—helpers, apprentices, salespeople who represent you alone, a bookkeeper who is a full-time member of your staff, and so forth. The formation of this relationship entails nothing more than an agreement on your side to hire someone and an agreement by that person to work. Although a written contract is not necessary, except in the case of employment for more than one year, I suggest that employment terms be put down in writing so that there is no misunderstanding later.

Employment Contracts

If the employment is to be for more than one year, there must be a written contract specifying the period of employment; otherwise, either party may terminate the relationship at any time. While there is no prescribed form that the contract must take, there are, nevertheless, certain items that should be considered. The first item of an employment contract is the term of employment. An employment contract may be either terminable at will or for a fixed duration. Making the contract for a fixed period gives the employee some job security and creates a moral and contractual obligation for the employee to remain for the term. Of course, if the employee chooses to quit, or the employer chooses to fire the employee, the law will not compel fulfillment of the contract. That went out with selling orphans into apprenticeships and other forms of slavery. Improper premature termination of a contract for a fixed period, however, will subject the party who is responsible for the wrongful act to liability for damages.

The second item is the wage. Unless you are a large employer with forty-five or more employees, or are engaged in interstate commerce (defined as having gross sales of $500,000 or more), you will not have to comply with federal minimum-wage laws. Most states, however, have their own minimum-wage laws with which you will still have to comply. Above the requirement imposed by this law, the amount of remuneration is open to bargaining.

In addition to an hourly wage or monthly salary, other benefits can be given, such as health and life insurance or retirement pensions. Some legal advice in this area may be necessary in order to take advantage of tax laws. In the event no salary is specified, the law will presume a reasonable wage for the work performed. Thus, you cannot escape paying your employees fairly by not discussing the amount they will earn. If you hire a mechanic and the accepted salary in your region for a qualified mechanic is $20 per hour, then it will be presumed that the mechanic was hired for this amount unless you and that person have agreed to a different salary.

Third, it is often wise to spell out your employee's duties in the employment contract. This serves as a form of orientation for the employee and also may limit future conflicts over what is and what is not involved in the job.

Fourth, you may want your employee to agree not to work for someone else while working for you or, more importantly, not to compete against you at the end of the employment period. The latter agreement must be carefully drawn to be enforceable. Such an agreement must not be overly broad in the kind of work the employee may not do; it must cover a geographic area no broader than that in which you actually operate; and it must be for a reasonable duration—a three-year period has been upheld. Note that some states impose restrictions on noncompetition agreements. In Oregon, for example, a noncompetition agreement is unenforceable unless it was entered into either prior to or contemporaneously with the beginning of employment—or unless it became effective after a meaningful promotion. Some states refuse to uphold noncompetition agreements. For example, California law states that a noncompetition agreement is void, as it is against public policy.

Employers may achieve some form of protection by restricting the use of the business's intellectual property. This should include a prohibition on the use of any company trade secrets, both during the term of employment and thereafter. These restrictions should be in writing. It has been held that trade secrets may include, among other things, customer lists, supplier lists, secret formulas, and know how.

Finally, grounds for termination of the employment contract should be listed, even if the contract is terminable at will. You should clearly specify that the contract may be terminated either for the specified causes or at the will of the employer.

Unlike the situation where you have hired an independent contractor, you are "vicariously liable" for the negligence and, sometimes, even the intentional wrongdoing of your employee when the employee is acting on your behalf. This means that if your employee is on the job and is involved in an automobile accident that is his or her fault, you, as well as your employee, are legally liable. It would be wise to be extremely careful when hiring, and to contact your insurance agent to obtain sufficient insurance coverage for your additional exposure.

Other Considerations in Hiring

There are other issues you should consider when hiring an employee, most of which fall into the realm of accounting or bookkeeping responsibilities. You should, therefore, consult with your accountant or bookkeeper regarding such items as the following:

1. A workers' compensation policy for your employees in the event of on-the-job injury or occupational illness. State laws vary on the minimum number of employees that triggers this very important requirement. The workers' compensation laws of many states provide that an employer who has failed to obtain or keep in force required workers' compensation insurance will be strictly liable even in the absence of negligence for on-the-job injury or illness. This includes not only medical expenses, but also damages for pain and suffering, lost earning potential, and other damages that are a consequence of on-the-job injuries or illnesses.

2. Withholding taxes (federal, state, and local). Here, too, the laws vary, and you must find out what is required in your locale.

3. Social Security (FICA). There are some exemptions from this body of social legislation. Contact your nearby Social Security office to determine how these exemptions may affect you.

4. Unemployment insurance (both federal and state). These also include certain technical requirements for subcontractors and the like.

5. Health and safety regulations (both federal and state).

6. Municipal taxes for specific programs such as schools or public transportation.

7. Employee benefits such as insurance coverage (medical, dental, prepaid legal), retirement benefits, memberships, and parking.

8. Union requirements if you or your employees are subject to union contracts.

9. Wage and hour laws (both federal and state). These include minimum wage and overtime requirements. In some states, the law also regulates holidays and vacations as well as the method of paying employees during employment and upon termination.

As already noted, the requirements of these laws may vary dramatically from state to state, and you are well advised to discuss them with your lawyer, accountant, and bookkeeper. In addition, you should find out if any other forms of employment legislation, such as licensing requirements, apply to you, your employees, or your business.

Hazards in the Workplace

On February 10, 1983, a sixty-one-year-old Polish-born employee of a film-recovery company in Chicago died of cyanide poisoning. He had worked for a small company that extracted silver from x-ray and photographic film. The work force consisted primarily of Polish immigrants and Mexican-American employees who spoke little English and were not very sophisticated.

To extract the silver, the film-recovery workers put the film in a vat containing cyanide and then transferred the film to a second vat that extracted the silver. The work was labor intensive and the vats were not properly vented and emitted dangerous fumes. Many of the employees complained of symptoms associated with cyanide poisoning, such as dizziness, nausea, and a bitter taste in the mouth. The employer made no efforts to warn them of the hazards of the work.

After the employee died and was examined by a county medical officer, it was determined that the cause of death was cyanide poisoning.

Government officials examined the plant where the employee had worked and found numerous health and safety violations. Eight months later, the president of the company and numerous corporate officials, as well as the company itself, were charged with and convicted of murder. The court concluded that the company, its officers, and directors were aware of the serious risk and hazards resulting from cyanide use, but they took no steps to alleviate the hazards in the plant. They did not even post warning signs that the foreign-born employees could understand.

While few manufacturers would intentionally injure a fellow human being, you may nevertheless find yourself in a similar situation. It is not uncommon to use toxic materials and to hire apprentices or employees in manufacturing. Employees are often not aware of the potential hazard that may result from the toxic materials. Unfortunately, few materials are labeled for toxicity. It is advisable to research the potentially toxic effects of all substances used in your process or product, whether or not they are labeled for toxicity. You should then disclose pertinent information regarding hazardous substances to your employees when they are hired.

Congress and federal administrative agencies are becoming more active in the field of regulation of hazardous substances. You should also be aware that your state workers' compensation agency or the Occupational Safety and Health Administration may have passed special rules regarding specific workplace substances and activities. It is critical to obtain a lawyer's opinion as to whether any of these regulations apply to your particular manu-facturing process or other business. Your state's labor department may also be able to give you information regarding applicable workplace regulations.

Many manufacturers of art and craft supplies have begun to voluntarily label their materials with health and safety warnings. Responding to pressure from art and craft advocate groups in 1979, the U.S. Congress even considered a federal law entitled the Federal Art Hazard Bill. After shuttling through several committees, however, it died in 1981.

Following the pattern established by the federal lobbyists, several states, including California and Oregon, recently did enact state art and craft labeling laws. Advocates of a healthy workplace are actively lobbying for similar laws throughout the United States.

Even though these laws are being enacted, your lawyer may not be able to tell you exactly to what extent you are legally obligated to advise your employees of potential risks inherent in their jobs. Again, the best course for an employer in doubt is to advise the newly hired individual of all known hazards that may result from the work and to disclose the fact that there may be other undiscovered risks in using the particular materials involved in creating the product. If an employment contract is used, a paragraph containing such a disclosure and the employee's acknowledgment of the known risks should be incorporated in the contract. A similar statement should also be included in any employment handbook.

While these documents would not provide a defense to a workers' compensation claim, they would sensitize employees to the need for caution in working with the toxic materials. Needless to say, you should take all precautions possible to protect the health and safety of your employees.

Termination of Employees

Determining whether someone is an employee or an independent contractor is not always easy. The reason that the characterization is important is that employers are responsible for income-tax withholding, Social Security, workers' compensation, and the like, whereas one who merely hires an independent contractor is not.

There is another reason that the characterization may be important. If the individual working for you is merely an independent contractor, the contract between you and that person will govern your respective rights of termination. On the other hand, if the individual is an employee, care must be taken not to become responsible for a wrongful termination when dismissing the individual.

Historically, an employee who was not under contract could be terminated for any reason whatsoever. Approximately thirty years ago, this right of absolute dismissal was challenged and the rule was modified. At that time, it was held that an employee could be terminated for the right reason or for no reason at all, but could not be terminated for the wrong reason. For example, an employee who was terminated for refusing to commit perjury before a legislative committee was entitled to recover against the employer for wrongful termination. The public policy of having individuals testify honestly was considered more important than the employer's right to control the employment relationship.

Courts have become even more protective of the rights of employees. In a 1983 case, *Novosel v. Nationwide Insurance Company,* the U.S. Circuit Court of Appeals held that the power to hire and fire could not be used to dictate an employee's political activity, and that even a nongovernment entity is limited by the Constitution in its power to discharge an employee. The court, in essence, held that one's right to exercise constitutionally protected free speech was more important than the employer's right to control an employee's conduct.

Wrongful termination cases fall into at least four general categories. Employers may not legally terminate an employee for the following reasons:

1. Refusing to commit an unlawful act, such as committing perjury or refusing to participate in illegal price-fixing schemes
2. Performing a public obligation, such as serving on a jury or serving in a military reserve unit
3. Exercising a statutory right, such as filing a claim for workers' compensation
4. Discrimination

In a bizarre case, the Arizona Supreme Court held that an employee who was terminated for refusing to "moon" fellow employees in a parody of the song "Moon River" during a company retreat was entitled to damage for wrongful termination. The public policy of protecting her right of privacy was deemed more important than the employer's right to terminate employees for disobedience. The courts appear to go quite far in holding that an employer cannot discharge an employee unless there is just cause for termination. A number of states have considered the adoption of legislation that would restrict the employer's right to terminate an employee to cases in which there was just cause. These laws also contain specific prohibitions on the termination of employees for "whistle-blowing," i.e., cases in which employees notify government authorities of wrongful acts by the employer, such as tax evasion, or cases in which employees tell corporate officers about wrongful acts of immediate supervisors.

Employers should take some precautions to avoid being placed in the untenable position of having bound themselves to individuals in their employment when the relationship has soured. This can result from language in employee handbooks, which might be construed as giving rise to a contractual right. It is also possible that oral statements made by recruiters or interviewers could give rise to contractual rights. To avoid this problem, an employer should have a legend placed in any employee handbook making it clear that the material is not an employment contract. It has also become common for employers to require prospective employees to sign a statement making it clear that the employment is at will and does not give rise to any contractual right. If there is a probationary period, the employer should be careful to state that the probationary employee will become a "regular" or "full-time" employee rather than a "permanent" employee. In addition, if there is any evaluation of the employee after the probationary period has ended, it should be conducted fairly. When evaluations become merely pro forma, problems can and do arise. Employees may argue that they have received sparkling evaluations and are being terminated for some invalid reason.

Perhaps an employer who uses evaluations should employ what has been characterized as progressive discipline. In this procedure, the employer starts by orally warning a problem employee of his or her concern and progressively imposing disciplinary practices until termination becomes the only form of recourse left. Care should be taken not to violate the employee's rights since the liability for wrongful termination can be catastrophic to a small business. When in doubt, an employer should contact an attorney with some experience in the field of employment relations. In this area, as with many others, preproblem counseling can prevent a good deal of time-consuming and costly litigation.

20 Keeping Taxes Low

A business can enhance profitability by increasing sales or by reducing expenses. Careful purchasing will go far in expense reduction, but one of the most profound areas affecting business conduct is tax. Prudent businesspeople are careful to determine the tax consequence of virtually every transaction, and most business planning is tax driven.

Periodic meetings with your business lawyer and tax accountant in order to determine the most expeditious and cost-effective method of conducting your business is important. I customarily advise my business clients to have at least one year-end planning session for the purpose of evaluating business activities and tax planning.

After allowing for basic needs through personal exemptions, a narrow list of personal deductions, and one reduced tax rate at the low end of the income scale, our income tax system is essentially a fixed-rate system. There are now five graduated tax rates for individuals: 15 percent on the lowest taxable income range, 28 percent and 31 percent on income in the middle taxable income ranges, and 36 percent and 39.6 percent on income in the highest taxable income ranges. Capital gains taxes for most investments held at least eighteen months were cut from 28 percent to 20 percent by the Taxpayer Relief Act of 1997. The act also adds a new 10 percent capital gains rate for taxpayers in the 15 percent tax bracket. Thus, individuals or organizations earning more money still generally pay a higher overall percentage of tax. In other respects, however, large and small businesses are treated alike by the Internal Revenue Service (IRS).

Income Spreading

There are two important means of reducing tax liability. The first is spreading taxable income by the use of several provisions in the tax code. The second is the use of deductions.

Income in Installments and Deferred Payments

One way a business can spread income is to receive payment in installments. Care must be taken with the mechanics of this arrangement. If a business sells a product for a negotiable note due in full at some future date or for some other deferred-payment obligation that is essentially equivalent to cash, or that has an ascertainable fair market value, the business may have to report the total proceeds of the sale as income realized when the note is received, not when the note is paid off with cash. (A *negotiable note* is a written and signed promise to pay a specified sum of money either on demand or at a specified time, payable either to an identified party or to the bearer.) However, the Internal Revenue Code (IRC) enables a taxpayer who sells property with payments received in successive tax years to report the income on an installment basis in some situations if the sale is properly structured. Under this method, tax is imposed only as payments are received.

For example, suppose you sell a custom-designed computer software package for $3,000. Ordinarily, the entire $3,000 would be taxable income in the year you received it. But if you use the installment method, with four payments of $750 plus interest received over four years, income from the sale will be taxed as the installments are received. In either case, the amount of income is $3,000, but under the installment method the amount is spread out over four years, and you are taking advantage of being in a lower tax bracket than had you taken the full $3,000 in the year you sold the software package. If, however, this were a standard software package, which would be characterized as inventory, the installment method would be unavailable. Be aware that there are special rules for installment sales, which should be discussed with your tax advisor.

Someone in a high tax bracket might wish to defer income until the future. For example, a commissioned salesperson could obtain an agreement from the employer that commissions paid would not exceed a certain amount in any one year, with the excess to be carried over and paid in the future. This would result in tax savings if, when the deferred amounts are finally paid, the salesperson were in a lower tax bracket.

There are drawbacks to deferred payments. These include the possibility that the party owing the money may not be willing to pay interest on the deferred sums and the possibility that that party could go broke before the debt is fully paid. One should consider these risks carefully before entering into a contract for deferred payments because it might be quite difficult to change the arrangement if the need should arise.

Spreading Income Among Family Members

Another strategy for business owners in high tax brackets is to divert some income directly to members of their immediate families who are in lower tax brackets, by hiring them as employees. Putting dependent children on the payroll can result in substantial tax savings because their salaries can be deducted as a business expense, but at the same time you are not required to withhold Social Security from the children's wages.

Your child can earn up to the amount of the standard deduction without any tax liability. You as the taxpayer can still claim a personal-dependency exemption for the child if you provide over half of his or her support. This salary arrangement is permissible so long as the child is under nineteen years of age or, if the child is between the ages of nineteen and twenty-four, is a full-time student. The child, however, may not claim a personal exemption if he or she can be claimed by the parents on their tax return.

The following are other restrictions on such an arrangement:

- The salary must be reasonable in relation to the child's age and the work performed
- The work performed must be a necessary service to the business
- The work must actually be performed by the child

A second method of transferring income to members of your family is the creation of a family partnership. Each partner receives an equal share of the overall income, unless the partnership agreement provides otherwise. The income is taxed once as individual income to each partner. Thus, if you are the parent who heads a family business, you can break up and divert your income to your family members, so it will be taxed to them according to their respective tax brackets. The income received by children may be taxed at significantly lower rates, resulting in more income reaching the family than if it had all been received by the parent, who is presumably in a higher tax bracket than the children. The law stipulates, however, that if a child is under fourteen years of age, and receives unearned income from the partnership, any amount over $1,300 will be taxed at the parents' highest marginal rate.

Although the IRS recognizes family partnerships, it may subject them to close scrutiny to ensure that the partnership is not a sham. In addition, because partnership capital produces significant income and partners are reasonably compensated for services performed for the partnership, the IRS may opt to forbid the shift in income, in accordance with the Internal Revenue Code section that deals with distribution of partners' shares and family partnerships. The same section provides that a person owning a capital interest (or ownership interest) in a family partnership will be considered a partner for tax purposes even if he or she received the capital interest as a gift, if the gift is genuine and irrevocable.

Incorporating a Family or Setting Up a Limited Liability Company [LLC]

Some families have even incorporated or created family-owned limited liability companies. If the IRS questions the motivation for such incorporation, the courts will examine the intent of the family members. If the sole purpose of incorporating was tax avoidance, the scheme will not stand. If the IRS successfully contends that the business entity should be disregarded, the IRS can reallocate income from the corporation or LLC to the individual taxpayer. This will be done, for example, if the corporation or LLC does not engage in substantial business activity and does not observe proper formalities or if its separate status is not otherwise adhered to by the businessperson.

Tax Advantages and Disadvantages

A bona fide (genuine) corporation or LLC being taxed as a corporation, however, may provide some tax advantages for the small-business owner. As an employee, the owner can control his or her taxable income with a limited salary and part or all of the income the entity receives from sales can be deferred. Although the corporation or LLC must recognize income whenever a sale is made, the corporation or LLC can deduct the owner's salary as well as other business expenses.

Nevertheless, incorporating or creating an LLC should not be done solely for tax reasons. The Tax Reform Act of 1986 reduced individual rates so that they are substantially in line with, or lower than, the entity rates for most taxpayers. Additionally, there are some unavoidable legal and accounting expenses that will have to be paid by the corporation or LLC. If your business operates on very small margins, you should determine if the possible tax savings to you justify the additional legal and accounting costs associated with corporations or LLCs. The cost to the entity of payroll taxes, unemployment taxes, workers' compensation, and legal and accounting fees can be substantial. In addition, use of the corporate form is no longer necessary for setting up a retirement plan. As discussed in chapter 23, revisions to the rules for pension plans allow a self-employed person to set aside as much money for retirement as could be done through a corporate retirement plan.

While creating a business entity may not provide tax benefits in some situations, and may even result in added expense, it still may afford you a liability shield. As I pointed out in chapter 1, many businesses are incorporated or created as LLCs for the sole purpose of obtaining limited liability for their owners, rather than for the tax treatment accorded business entities.

Moreover, there are several potential business tax problems that the businessperson should carefully consider before incorporating. Making use of a corporate form means that any distribution of profits to shareholders in the form of dividends will be taxed twice: once at the entity level as business income and again at the shareholder level as personal income when profits are distributed to the shareholders or owner. Thus, although incorporation allows income to be shifted from the businessperson to other shareholders, such as family members, the shift occurs at the expense of double taxation. Obviously, it is important to consult with a CPA or tax advisor in order to determine whether the benefit of shifting income to a corporation outweighs the effects of double taxation.

Another alternative for the small enterprise is to organize as an S corporation and be taxed as a sole proprietor or partnership. S corporation classification allows the owners to elect to be taxed much like a partnership and thus avoid double taxation. (The S corporation is discussed in chapter 1.)

The tax law allows LLCs to elect to be taxed as entities (identical to regular or C corporations) or to be taxed as if the business were still run as a sole proprietorship (in states allowing one-person LLCs) or partnership. You should be aware that some states have a gross receipts tax for LLCs, which may make an LLC an unattractive option in your state. LLCs are discussed more fully in chapter 1.

Taxes on Accumulated Earnings and Passive Investment Income

If a person incorporates in order to postpone a significant portion of income, the IRS may impose an accumulated-earnings tax. However, the Internal Revenue Code allows a maximum accumulation of $250,000, which is not subject to the accumulated-earnings tax. For corporations whose principal work is in the fields of health, law, engineering, architecture, accounting, actuarial science, performing arts, or consulting, the maximum is $150,000. Accumulated earnings beyond these maximums must be justified as reasonable for the needs of the business. Otherwise, they will be subject to a tax of 39.6 percent, in addition to the regular corporate tax.

The IRC also imposes an additional tax on most types of *passive investment income,* which is income retained by the corporation or LLC if the business entity is found to be a personal holding company. The current rate is 39.6 percent. This may occur if a majority of the corporation's income consists of copyright, book, movie, or other royalties; dividends; rents; or personal-service contracts.

Also, if the owner sells his or her stock or ownership interest before the corporation has realized any income, the corporation could become a *collapsible corporation*, causing the gain realized on the sale of the stock to be taxed at ordinary income rates.

Qualifying for Business Deductions

Up until now, I have been discussing the various ways in which business owners can spread their taxable incomes or can take advantage of lower tax rates by incorporating. Another means of reducing tax liability involves making use of deductions. For this, you must keep full and accurate records. Receipts are a necessity. Even if your business is homebased, as are many start-up businesses, you should have a separate checking account and a complete set of books for all the activities of your trade or business. A hobbyist or dilettante is not entitled to trade or business deductions, except in very limited circumstances.

Tax laws presume that a person is engaged in a business or trade, as opposed to a hobby, if a net profit results from the activity in question during three out of the five consecutive years ending with the taxable year in question (or, in the case of horse breeding, training, or racing, two out of the seven consecutive years ending with the taxable year in question). For instance, if the freelance writer, artist, or craftsperson does not have three profitable years in the last five years of working as such, the IRS may contend that the work merely constitutes a hobby. In this case, the taxpayer will have to prove *profit motive* in order to claim business expenses. Proof of profit motive does not require proof that a profit would actually be made; it requires proof only of intention to make a profit.

The Treasury regulations call for an objective standard on the profit-motive issue, so statements of the taxpayer as to intent will not suffice as proof. The regulations list the following nine factors to be used in determining profit motive:

1. The manner in which the taxpayer carries on the activity (e.g., effective business routines and bookkeeping procedures)
2. The expertise of the taxpayer or the taxpayer's advisors (e.g., study in an area, awards, prior publication, critical recognition, and membership in professional organizations)

3. The time and effort expended in carrying on the activity (i.e., at least several hours a day devoted to the activity, preferably on a regular basis)
4. Expectation that business assets will increase in value
5. The success of the taxpayer in similar or related activities (e.g., past successes, even if prior to the relevant five-year period)
6. History of income or losses with respect to the activity (e.g., increases in receipts from year to year, unless losses vastly exceed receipts over a long period of time)
7. The amount of occasional profits, if any, that are earned
8. Financial status (wealth sufficient to support a hobby would weigh against the profit motive)
9. Elements of personal pleasure or recreation (if significant traveling is involved and little work accomplished, the court may be suspicious of profit motive)

No single factor will determine the results. The 1928 case of *Deering v. Blair* provides an example of how the factors are used. Deering was the executor of the estate of Reginald Vanderbilt, whose financial affairs and residence were in New York. Vanderbilt had purchased a farm near Portsmouth, Rhode Island, because he was interested in horses, and operated it as a business. The business produced little income, but Vanderbilt claimed business expenses of over $25,000 in each of three years. The fact that Vanderbilt did not rely on the income from the farm for his livelihood was considered by the court in making its decision. The court held that, despite the fact that he had several employees and advertised the farm's horse-boarding and rental services, the purpose for operating the farm was not to produce a profit. Rather, the land was used for pleasure, entertaining, exhibition, and social diversion. Thus, the business deduction was disallowed.

While a new business is not presumed to be "engaged in for profit" until it shows a profit three out of five years (or, where applicable, two out of seven years), deductions have been allowed in cases where this test is not met. In *Allen v. Commissioner,* the tax court decided to allow business deductions for the proprietors of a ski lodge that was rented out during the ski season. The deduction was allowed even though the lodge did not show a profit during the years in question and despite the fact that the proprietors did not depend on the income from the lodge for their livelihood. They did, however, keep accurate records and did not use the lodge for their personal pleasure. Consequently, they were able to show that the lodge was operated as a business.

In *Engdahl v. Commissioner,* the tax court found a profit motive on the part of the taxpayers who were considering retirement and wanted to supplement their incomes by operating a horse ranch. The court held that, despite a series of losses, the taxpayers had kept complete and accurate records reviewed by an accountant, had advertised the operation, took their horses to shows, and had worked up to fifty-five hours per week on the operation. Additionally, the assets of the ranch had appreciated in value. All these facts showed that the taxpayers had a profit motive and, therefore, the business-expense deductions were allowed.

Once you have established yourself as engaged in a business, all your ordinary and necessary expenditures for that business are deductible business expenses. This would include materials and supplies, workspace, office equipment, research or professional books and magazines, travel for business purposes, certain conference fees, any agent commissions, postage, legal fees, and accountant fees.

One of the most significant and problematic of these deductible expenses is the workspace deduction. It is not uncommon for smaller businesses to be based at home for a variety of reasons, the most important of which is probably economic. The cost of renting a separate office is such that many small-business owners, especially in the start-up phase, are unwilling or unable to pay it. Others, of course, choose to work at home because it enables them to juggle work and family. Whatever the reason, taxpayers who wish to claim deductions for use of their homes in their business will have to do some careful planning.

Deductions for the Use of a Home in Business

For some time, the IRS did not allow deductions for offices or studios in homes. This policy was challenged in a case in which a physician managed rental properties as a sideline. The doctor's rental business was run out of an office in his house, and the space was used only for this particular business. When the physician deducted the expenses for the office in his home, the IRS disallowed the deduction. But the court was apparently convinced by the physical set-up of the room that the doctor used it exclusively and regularly as an office in connection with his rental business. The court noted the room had no television set, sofa, or bed.

This decision now has been incorporated into the tax code. As a general rule, a business deduction is not allowed for the use of a dwelling that is used by the taxpayer during the taxable year as a residence. (There are some technical rules regarding qualification of a dwelling as a residence.) The tax code makes an exception to this general rule in certain circumstances. The taxpayer is allowed to take a deduction for a portion of a dwelling unit "exclusively used on a regular basis . . . as a principal place of business for any trade or business of the taxpayer," even if that business is not the taxpayer's primary source of income.

Exclusive and Regular Use

The exclusive and regular use exception applies to any portion of the residence used *exclusively* and *on a regular basis* as the owner's *principal place* of conducting that business. The qualifications for this exception are strictly construed by the IRS and the courts. The requirement of exclusivity means that the taxpayer may not mix personal use and business use. In other words, an office that doubles as a storeroom for personal belongings, a laundry room, guest bedroom, or the like will not qualify as an office for tax purposes, and a taxpayer may not deduct such space as an office.

However, there has been a recent liberalization of this rule in some parts of the country where the courts have held that a studio or an office can exist in a room that has a personal use, so long as a clearly defined area is used exclusively for business. It is important to remember that generally the Internal Revenue Service functions on a regional basis. Except for issues that have been reserved for decision by the national office, each IRS office is independent and makes its own decisions until the U.S. Supreme Court or Congress makes a decision that applies nationally. This is why the decision by a circuit court in one area may not apply elsewhere.

The requirement regarding regular use means that the use of the room may not be merely incidental or occasional. Obviously, there is a gray area between regular and occasional use. Perhaps some business owners just starting up can use this rule as an inducement to overcome temporary bouts of laziness or ennui. For if you are planning on deducting any expenses for your office, you must keep working to satisfy the regularity test.

Like the regularity requirement, the rule regarding the principal place of business has been vague and interpreted differently. In *Meiers v. Commissioner,* the plaintiff owned a self-service laundromat. Mrs. Meiers managed the business, supervised the five part-time employees, and performed other managerial and bookkeeping functions. She spent only about an hour a day at the laundromat and two hours a day in her office at home. The office was used exclusively for activities related to business. The tax court ruled that since the laundromat was the "focal point" of the business, any deduction for an office in the home should be disallowed.

The Court of Appeals for the Seventh Circuit reversed that decision, holding that rather than using the focal point of the business as the basis of its decision, the tax court should have looked to the principal place of the taxpayer's activities. Managerial decisions were made from the office and a conscious decision was made *not* to create an office at the laundromat itself. For these reasons, the office-at-home deduction was allowed.

In 1993, however, the Supreme Court held in *Soliman v. Commissioner* that home-office deductions were not available where the taxpayer performed the services or delivered goods outside of the home and income was not directly generated at home.

The Taxpayer Relief Act of 1997 expands the definition of a taxpayer's principal place of business to include the place where administrative and management activities are conducted, if there is no other fixed location for the accomplishment of such tasks, effective in 1999. For instance, an artist who creates artwork in a rented studio space could take the deduction for an office at home if the administrative aspects of the business, such as contacting galleries regarding sales and ordering supplies, were conducted from the home office.

In another case, the tax court disallowed a claim for an office-at-home deduction despite a unique argument. In *Baie v. Commissioner,* the taxpayers operated a hot-dog stand some distance from their home. Because the stand measured only ten feet by ten feet, some of the food preparation and storage was done at home. The ruling by the tax court was based on the fact that the kitchen and storage areas were not used exclusively for business purposes. The taxpayers used the argument that they were actually engaged in a manufacturing operation at home and, therefore, the office-at-home section of the IRC did not apply. The court held that the statute included such an operation and the deduction was not allowed.

Another tax-court decision denying the office-at-home deduction was *Moller v. United States.* The taxpayers were a husband and wife who claimed a deduction for the area of their home used to manage their investments. The court held that in order to qualify as a trade or business, the business must consist of the active buying and selling of securities, with income derived therefrom. The Mollers, however, derived their income from the dividends and interest resulting from holding securities for a long time. This, the court held, did not rise to the level of carrying on a trade or business.

When the office is in a structure separate from the principal residence, the requirements for deductibility are less stringent. The structure must be used exclusively and on a regular basis, just as an office in the home. However, when the office is in a separate structure, it need only be used "in connection with" the business, not as the principal place of business.

When taxpayers use a portion of their homes for storage of business materials (as well as for business), the requirements for deductibility of the storage area are also less stringent. The dwelling must be the sole fixed location of the business, and the storage area must be used on a regular basis for the storage of the business equipment or products. The room used for storage need not be used entirely or exclusively for business, but there must be a "separately identifiable space suitable for storage" of the business-related materials.

Is the Office-at-Home Deduction Worthwhile?

If a taxpayer meets one of the tests outlined above, the next question is what tax benefits can result. The answer after close analysis is frequently, Not very many. An *allocable portion* of mortgage interest and property taxes can be deducted against the business. These would be deductible anyway as itemized deductions. The advantage of deducting them against the business is that this reduces the business profit that is subject to self-employment taxes. Of course, a taxpayer who lives in a rented house and otherwise qualifies for the office-at-home deductions may deduct a portion of the rent that would not otherwise be tax deductible.

The primary tax advantage comes from a deduction for an allocable portion of repairs, utility bills, and depreciation. Otherwise, these would not be deductible at all. The allocable portion is the square footage of the space used for the business, divided by the total square footage of the house, and multiplied by your mortgage interest, property taxes, etc. Determining the amount of allowable depreciation is highly complex and you should discuss it with your accountant or tax advisor.

The total amount that can be deducted for an office or storage place in the home is artificially limited. The amount that can be deducted is determined by taking the total amount of money earned in the business and subtracting the allocable portion of mortgage interest and property taxes and other deductions allocable to the business. The remainder is the maximum amount that you can deduct for the allocable portion of repairs, utilities, and depreciation. In other words, your total business deductions in this situation cannot be greater than your total business income minus all other business expenses. The office-at-home deduction, therefore, cannot be used to create a net loss, but disallowed losses can be carried forward indefinitely and deducted in future years against profits from the business.

Besides the obvious complexity of the rules and the mathematics, there are several other factors that limit the benefit of taking a deduction for a studio or office in the home. One of these is the partial loss of the *nonrecognition of gain* (tax-deferred) treatment that is otherwise allowed when a taxpayer sells a personal residence. The Taxpayer Relief Act of 1997 allows homeowners to exclude up to $250,000 of gain ($500,000 for joint filers) from income with some restrictions. This deferral of gain, however, is not allowed to the extent that the house was used in the business. This means that the taxpayer must pay tax on the allocable portion of the gain from the sale.

For example, if you have been claiming 20 percent of your home as a business deduction, you will enjoy a tax deferral on only 80 percent of the profit from selling the home. The other 20 percent will be subject to tax because that 20 percent represents the sale of a business asset. In essence, for the price of a current deduction, you may be converting what is essentially a nonrecognition, or tax-deferred, asset into a trade or business property.

Some of that gain may be excluded if you have both (1) owned the home for two of the last five years, and (2) used the home exclusively for personal use for two of the last five years. If both requirements are met, tax must be paid only on the amount actually deducted for depreciation. If you plan to sell your home anytime soon, you should confer with an accountant or tax advisor.

Another concern is that by deducting for an office in the home, the taxpayer effectively puts a red flag on the tax return. Obviously, when the tax return expressly asks if expenses are being deducted for an office in the home, the question is not being asked for purely academic reasons. Although only the IRS knows how much the answer to this question affects someone's chances of being audited, there is no doubt that a "yes" answer does increase the likelihood of an audit.

Given this increased possibility of audit, it doesn't pay to deduct for an office in the home in doubtful situations. Taxpayers who lose the deduction must pay back taxes plus interest or fight in court. If you believe that your office at home could qualify for the business deduction, you would be well advised to consult with a competent tax expert who can assist in calculating the deduction.

Other Professional Expenses

As mentioned earlier, deductible business expenses include not only the workspace, but all the ordinary and necessary expenditures involved in the business. *Current expenses,* items with a useful life of less than one year, are fully deductible in the year incurred. Writing utensils and stationery, postage, and telephone bills are all examples of current expenses.

Many expenses, however, cannot be fully deducted in the year of purchase but can be depreciated. These kinds of costs are called *capital expenditures.* For example, the cost of equipment, such as a typewriter, computer, word processor, or pickup truck, all of which have useful lives of more than one year, are capital expenditures and cannot be fully deducted in the year of purchase. Instead, the taxpayer must depreciate, or allocate, the cost of the item over the estimated useful life of the asset. Although the actual useful life of professional equipment will vary, fixed periods have been established in the tax code over which depreciation may be deducted.

In some cases, it may be difficult to decide whether an expense is a capital expenditure or a current expense. Repairs to machinery are one example. If you spend $200 repairing your delivery van, this expense may or may not constitute a capital expenditure. The general test is determining whether the amount spent restoring the vehicle adds to its value or substantially prolongs its useful life. Since the cost of replacing short-lived parts of a vehicle to keep it in efficient working condition does not substantially add to its useful life, such a cost would be a current cost and would be deductible. The cost of rebuilding your van's engine, on the other hand, significantly extends its useful life. Thus, such a cost is a capital expenditure and must be depreciated.

For many small businesses, an immediate deduction can be taken when equipment is purchased. In 1998, up to $18,000 of such purchases may be "expensed" for the year and need not be depreciated at all. This amount will increase to $25,000 by 2003.

Commissions paid to salespeople, as well as fees paid to lawyers or accountants for business purposes, are generally deductible as current expenses. The same is true of salaries paid to others whose services are necessary for the business. If you need to hire help, it is a good idea to hire people on an individual-project basis as independent contractors rather than as regular employees. This avoids your having to pay Social Security, disability, and withholding-tax payments on their accounts. You should specify the job-by-job basis of the assignments, detail when each project is to be completed and, if possible, allow the person you are hiring to choose the place to do the work. If there is any doubt about whether an individual is actually an independent contractor, contact a skilled employment-law attorney, since the IRS could characterize the invidivual as an employee. In that event, you will be responsible for tax withholding and paying FICA taxes. In addition, problems may arise with respect to your pension plan.

Travel Expenses

On a business trip, whether within the United States or abroad, your ordinary and necessary expenses, including travel and lodging, may be

100 percent deductible if your travel is solely for business purposes, except for "luxury water travel." Business meals and meals consumed while on a business trip are deductible up to 50 percent of the actual cost. If the trip primarily involves a personal vacation, you can deduct business-related expenses at the destination, but you may not deduct the transportation costs.

If the trip is primarily for business but part of the time is given to a personal vacation, you must indicate which expenses are for business and which for pleasure. In such cases, a portion of the *business*-related expenses will be nondeductible. This is *not* true in the case of foreign trips if one of the following exceptions applies:

- You had no substantial control over arranging the trip
- Less than 25 percent of the time is spent in nonbusiness activity
- The trip outside the United States was for a week or less
- A personal vacation was not a major consideration in making the trip

If you are claiming one of these exceptions, you should be careful to have supporting documentation. If you cannot take advantage of one of the exceptions, you must allocate expenses for the trip abroad according to the percentage of the trip devoted to business as opposed to vacation.

The definition of what constitutes "a business stay" can be very helpful to the taxpayer in determining a trip's deductibility. Travel days, including the day of departure and the day of return, count as business days if travel outside the United States is for more than seven days and business activities occurred on such days. Any day that the taxpayer spends on business counts as a business day, even if only a part of the day is spent on business. A day in which business is canceled through no fault of the taxpayer counts as a business day. Saturdays, Sundays, and holidays count as business days even though no business is conducted, provided that business is conducted on the Friday before and the Monday after the weekend, or on one day on either side of the holiday.

Entertainment Expenses

Entertainment expenses incurred for the purpose of developing an existing business are also deductible in the amount of 50 percent of actual cost. However, you must be especially careful about recording entertainment expenses. You should record in your logbook the amount, date, place, type of entertainment, business purpose, substance of the discussion, the participants in the discussion, and the business relationship of the parties who are being entertained. Keep receipts for any expenses over $75. You should also keep in mind the stipulation in the tax code that disallows deductibility for expenses that are "lavish or extravagant under the circumstances." No guidelines have yet been developed as to the definition of the term "lavish or extravagant," but one should be aware of the restriction nevertheless. If tickets to a sporting, cultural, or other entertainment event are purchased, only the face value of the ticket is allowed as a deduction. If a skybox or other luxury box seat is purchased or leased and is used for business entertaining, the maximum deduction now allowed is 50 percent of the cost of a nonluxury box seat.

Expenses that the IRS Scrutinizes

The above rules cover business travel and entertainment expenses both inside and outside the United States. The rules are more stringent for expenses incurred while attending conventions and conferences outside the United States. Also, the IRS tends to review very carefully any deductions for attendance at business seminars that also involve a family vacation, whether inside the United States or abroad. In order to deduct the business expense, the taxpayer must be able to show, with documents, that the reason for attending the meeting was to promote production of income. Normally, for a spouse's expenses to be deductible, the spouse must be a co-owner or employee of the business. Often, seminars will offer special activities for husbands and wives that will provide documentation later on.

As a general rule, the business deductions are allowed for conventions and seminars held in North America. The IRS is taking a closer look at cruise ship seminars and is requiring two statements to be attached to the tax return. The first statement substantiates the number of days on the ship, the number of hours spent each day on business, and the activities in the program. The second statement must come from the sponsor of the convention to verify the initial information. In addition, the ship must be registered in the United States, and all ports of call must be located in the

United States or its possessions. The deduction is also limited to $2,000 per individual per year. Again, the key for the taxpayer taking this sort of deduction is careful documentation and substantiation.

What Goes into a Logbook

Keeping a logbook or expense diary is probably the best line of defense for the businessperson with respect to business expenses incurred while traveling. If you are on the road, keep the following things in mind:

With respect to travel expenses:
- Keep proof of the costs
- Record the time of departure
- Record the number of days spent on business
- List the places visited and the business purposes of your activities

With respect to the transportation costs:
- Keep copies of all receipts in excess of $75, and, if traveling by car, keep track of mileage
- Log all other expenses in your diary

Similarly, with meals, tips, and lodging, keep receipts for all items over $75 and make sure to record all less expensive items in your logbook.

Businesspersons may also take tax deductions for their attendance at workshops, seminars, retreats, and the like, provided they are careful to document the business nature of the trip. Accurate recordkeeping is the first line of defense for tax preparation. Note that it is no longer possible to deduct for investment seminars or conventions, as opposed to business conventions.

Charitable Deductions

The law provides that an individual or business can donate either money or property to qualified charities and take a tax deduction for the donation. Individuals are afforded more favorable deductions for donations of money or property they own than are artists donating their own creations or businesspeople who donate property out of their inventories.

The tax law requires independent appraisals of property donated in a form prescribed in the IRC. In addition, if the taxpayer receives any benefit from the charity, the amount deducted must be by the fair market value of the benefit received. Benefits could include, for example, attendance at museum openings, merchandise such as books, tapes, or CDs.

Since this area can be quite technical, you should consult with your tax advisor before making any charitable donations. In addition, there have been some abuses on the part of charities that resulted in misappropriations of donated funds. If you have any question about the validity of a particular charity, you should contact your state attorney general's office or the local governmental agency that polices charitable solicitations in your area.

Grants, Prizes, and Awards

Individuals who receive income from grants or fellowships should be aware that this income can be excluded from gross income and thus represents considerable tax savings. For an individual to qualify for this exclusion, the grant must be for the purpose of furthering his or her education and training. However, amounts received under a grant or fellowship that are specifically designated to cover expenses related to the grant are no longer fully deductible. Furthermore, if the grant is given as compensation for services or is primarily for the benefit of the grant-giving organization, it cannot be excluded.

For scholarships and fellowships granted after August 16, 1986, the deduction is allowed only if the recipient is a degree candidate. The amount of the exclusion from income is limited to the amounts used for tuition, fees, books, supplies, and equipment. Amounts designated for room, board, and other incidental expenses are included in income. No exclusion from income is allowed for recipients who are not degree candidates.

The above rules apply to income from grants and fellowships. Unfortunately, the Tax Reform Act of 1986 also put tighter restrictions on money, goods, or services received as prizes or awards. Previously, the amounts received for certain awards were excluded from income if the recipient was rewarded for past achievements and had not applied for the award. Examples of this type of award are the Pulitzer Prize and the Nobel

Prize. Under the present law, any prizes or awards for religious, charitable, scientific, or artistic achievements are included as income to the recipient unless the prize is assigned to charity.

Health Insurance

Self-employed individuals may deduct a percentage of the amount paid for medical insurance for themselves, their spouses, and their dependents. The percentage is 45 percent in 1998 and 1999. This amount will gradually increase to 100 percent by 2007.

If you do not know whether a particular activity is deductible, you should consult with a competent CPA or tax advisor before embarking on it. In any case, consultation with qualified tax professionals is always advisable to ensure maximum benefits.

21

Are You Zoned to Work at Home?

It is common for the small-business owner to have an office or workshop in a home or garage. The problems raised by the multiple use of a dwelling can be divided into two basic areas: whether local zoning regulations legally allow working and living in the same place, and whether the income tax laws recognize the realities of business start-ups. For a full discussion of the income tax considerations of designating a part of your home as an office, see the previous chapter. In this chapter, I will discuss the problem of zoning.

Local Zoning Restrictions

For the person who wants to live and work in the same space, local zoning ordinances can be a significant issue. Some city ordinances flatly prohibit using the same space as a business and as a dwelling. In some commercially zoned areas where low-cost lofts and studios are available, it is illegal to maintain a residence in the same space. In residential areas, regulations may require permits and restrict the size and use of the workspace. Since municipal and county ordinances vary, the business owner should check with the appropriate local government agency to determine specific requirements. The fire department, for example, would undoubtedly have to approve the use of a kiln.

For the person who wants to maintain an office or workshop in the garage or basement of a residence, several types of restrictions may apply. The space devoted to the work activity may be limited to a certain number of square feet; outbuildings may or may not be allowed. The type of equipment used may also be restricted. Noise, smoke, and odor restrictions may apply, and approval may be required from all or some of the neighbors. If remodeling is contemplated, building codes must, of course, also be considered.

You also may have to obtain a home-occupation permit or, in many areas, a business license. The application fee for either of these will normally be a flat fee or a percentage of annual receipts from the activity. Depending upon the success of the business, this could become a substantial expense. In addition, your homeowner's or renter's insurance policy may contain some restrictions relating to commercial activity. You should contact your insurance broker to find out whether or not your policy contains such limitations and what can be done to deal with them.

In commercially zoned areas, small manufacturers may have more flexibility in the types of activities they conduct, particularly if they produce noise or odors that would be offensive to others in a residentially zoned location. But if you also wish to use the workspace for eating and sleeping, zoning ordinances may prohibit such use.

Some cities have recognized the hardships these zoning ordinances create for artists and craftspeople. In New York City, a municipal dwelling law was enacted exempting artists and their families from restrictions against living and working in the same apartment unit. The state of California also enacted legislation that grants local municipalities the right to adopt zoning ordinances that would accommodate artists who live in industrially or commercially zoned areas; other states have followed this pattern of multiple-use zoning.

While these laws have solved the immediate problem of artists and craftspeople living and working in the same location, new problems have been created. Once it became possible for artists to live and work in the Soho district of New York City, for example, the area became a magnet for galleries, boutiques, restaurants, and tourists. Many artists remain, but skyrocketing rents and prices have forced many others out. Before Soho became fashionable, no new industry could be enticed into the area. Consequently, landlords were pleased to have artists leasing their commercial properties. Once development caught on, however, buildings changed hands more often, and artists and craftspeople who had invested substantial sums in their lofts found that their commercial leases afforded them little protection.

A 1979 New York case, *Mandel v. Pitkowsky,* may provide residential loft tenants with some degree of security. Pitkowsky and sculptor Ulrich Niemeyer rented commercial quarters for ten years. Their lease limited their occupancy to an artist's studio. Nevertheless, their landlord encouraged them to convert the studio into their residence. Both sides were happy to abide by this illegal arrangement, apparently secure in the knowledge that the city was not diligently inspecting these properties. (This same pattern is now occurring in the Pearl District of my hometown, Portland, Oregon.)

When the lease expired, the landlord demanded a threefold increase in the rent. The landlord claimed that because the property was commercial rather than residential, it was not subject to the city's rent-stabilization laws. The court did not agree; the landlord's express approval of the tenants' ten-year residency converted the studio into a de facto multiple dwelling for purposes of the rent-stabilization laws.

Federal Regulations

Additional regulations that can adversely affect those who want to work at home are federal laws that inhibit cottage industries. The U.S. Department of Labor is actively enforcing a 1943 regulation that forbids individuals from producing in their homes for profit the following six categories of goods: embroidery, women's apparel, gloves and mittens, buttons and buckles, jewelry, and handkerchiefs.

The regulation was originally enacted many years ago when the Department of Labor found that minimum-wage violations were widespread in industries in which working at home predominated. The minimum wage is mandated by the federal Fair Labor Standards Act and requires employers to pay their employees no less than a set hourly rate. Overtime, at one-and-one-half times the employee's hourly rate, is also mandated for hours worked over forty hours per week.

In 1981, the department proposed repealing all regulations that prohibited cottage industries, but bitter labor union opposition resulted in the continuation of the regulation for all the targeted crafts except knitted outerwear, and even that exemption is still being considered in the courts.

The remaining regulations may create serious difficulties for people who want to work at home. In recent years, the disputes between labor unions, principally the International Ladies Garment Workers Union, and women who make their livings from cottage industries have become quite heated. The unions argue that they merely want to prevent sweatshop conditions, but many people believe that the real issue is nonunionized home labor competing with union members who work in unionized factories.

In order to fall within the scope of the regulation, the worker must be an employee. This does not mean, however, that a person can avoid the effect of the regulation simply by labeling him- or herself an independent contractor. Under the Fair Labor Standards Act, the test of employment is the economic reality of the relationship.

For example, the Supreme Court has held that members of a cooperative are employees for the purposes of the home-worker regulation. The decision was based on several factors including the fact that the cooperative's management decides the work to be performed and who is to do it. The management also decides who can become a member of the cooperative, and can terminate the relationship if a member's work is substandard.

At the other end of the spectrum are manufacturers who are self-employed and independent, selling their products on the open market, at wholesale or retail, for whatever price they can command. In this situation, the federal regulations do not apply. But for some people, the 1943 regulation poses a serious difficulty in living and working at home.

22 Renting Commercial Space

At some point in the life of your business, you will probably find it necessary to evaluate the terms and conditions of a commercial lease. Commercial leases are much more subject to negotiation and pitfalls than residential leases, which are more tightly regulated in most states. You should consult an attorney with experience in negotiating commercial leases before signing one.

Landlords typically employ the services of a broker when attempting to rent commercial space. In addition, many businesspeople hire brokers to assist them with lease negotiations. This discussion is intended to alert you to some of the topics that should arise in your discussion with your lawyer or real estate broker.

To begin with, the exact space to be rented should be spelled out in detail in the lease. Determine whether there is a distinction between the space leased and the actual space that is usable. Often, tenants are required to pay rent on commercial space measured from "wall to wall," though after the area is built out, the resulting usable space may be significantly smaller. If your space is in a shopping center and you share responsibility for common areas with other tenants, these responsibilities should be explained. Will you be responsible for cleaning and maintaining them, or will the landlord? When will the common areas be open or closed? What other facilities, such as restrooms and storage, are available to you?

Another important item is the cost of the space. Will you be paying a flat monthly rental or one that will change based on your earnings at the location, as is often the case when stores lease space in a shopping center? In order to evaluate the cost of the space, you should compare it with other similar spaces in the same locale. Do not be afraid to negotiate for more favorable terms. Care should be taken not to sign a lease that will restrict you from opening another facility close to the one being rented.

It is also important for you to consider the period of the lease. If, for example, you are merely renting a booth at a trade show, then you are only concerned with a short term. On the other hand, if you intend to rent for a year or two, it is a good idea to get an option to extend the lease because when you advertise and promote your business, your location is one of the things about which you will be telling people. Moving can cause a lot of problems with mail and telephone numbers. Besides, if you move every year or two, some customers may feel that you are unstable, and customers who buy on an irregular basis may not know where to find you after the lease period ends. Worse still, they may find a competitor in your old space.

Long-term leases are recordable in some states. Recording, where permitted, is generally accomplished by having the lease filed in the same office as a deed to the property would be filed. Check with a local real estate title company or real estate attorney for the particulars in your state. If you are in a position to record your lease, it is probably a good idea to do so since you will then be entitled to receive notices, legal and otherwise, which are related to the property.

It is essential for you to determine whether there are any restrictions on the particular activity you wish to perform on the leased premises. For example, the area may be zoned so as to prohibit you from manufacturing. It is a good idea to insist on a provision that puts the burden of obtaining any permit or variances on the landlord or, if you are responsible for them, the inability to obtain them should be grounds for terminating the lease without penalty.

Be sure the lease provides that you are permitted to use any sign or advertising on the premises, or spells out any restrictions. It is not uncommon, for example, for historic-landmark laws to regulate signs on old buildings. Can you put a sign in your window or in front of your building? Some zoning laws prohibit this.

You should also be aware that extensive remodeling may be necessary for certain spaces to become suitable for your use. If this is the case, then it is important for you to determine who will be responsible for the costs of remodeling. In addition, it is essential to find out whether it will be necessary for you to restore the premises to their original, preremodeled condition when the lease ends. This can be expensive and, in some instances, impossible. The Americans with Disabilities Act (ADA) of 1990 requires places of public accommodation to be reasonably accessible. The law is broadly interpreted and includes virtually every form of business. The term *reasonable accommodation* is not precise and thus it is important to determine what must be done in order to fulfill the requirements of this federal statute. Typically, approximately 25 percent of the cost of any covered remodel must be allocated to items that aid accessibility. These would include, among other things, levered door openers, Braille signs, larger bathroom stalls, wheelchair ramps, approved disability-accessible doors, and elevators. You should determine whether the cost of complying with the ADA will be imposed on the landlord, the tenant, or divided.

Who Pays for What?

If you need special hookups, such as water or electrical lines, you should determine whether the landlord will provide them or whether you will have to bear the cost. Of course, if the leased premises already have the necessary facilities, you should question the landlord regarding the cost of these utilities. Are they included in the rent or are they to be paid separately?

In some locations, garbage pickup is not a problem since it is one of the services provided by the municipality. On the other hand, it is common for renters to be responsible for their own trash disposal. In commercial spaces, this can be quite expensive and should be addressed in the lease.

Customarily, the landlord will be responsible for the exterior of the building. It will be the landlord's obligation to make sure that it does not leak during rainstorms and that it is properly ventilated. Notwithstanding this fact, it is important for you to make sure the lease deals with the question of responsibility if, for example, the building is damaged and some of your work or equipment is damaged or destroyed. Will you have to take out insurance for the building as well as its contents, or will the landlord assume responsibility for the building insurance?

Similarly, you should find out whether or not it will be your obligation to obtain liability insurance for injuries that are caused in portions of the building not under your control, such as common hallways and stairwells. You should, of course, have your own liability policy for accidental injuries or accidents that occur on your leased premises.

Security and Zoning

A good lease will also contain a provision dealing with security. If you are renting indoor space in a shopping center, it is likely that the landlord will be responsible for external security, although this is not universally the case. If you are renting an entire building, it is customarily your responsibility to provide whatever security you deem important. Does the lease permit you to install locks or alarm systems? If this is something in which you are interested, you should address the question.

Does the lease have any restrictions on deliveries, their time, or location? If you are dealing with large bulky items and are accepting deliveries or making them, your lease should contain a provision that will give you the flexibility you desire.

If the place you wish to rent will be used as both your personal dwelling and for business, other problems may arise. It is quite common for zoning laws to prohibit certain forms of commercial activities when the area is zoned residential (see chapter 21). You should consult with your attorney before attempting to operate out of your home.

Finally, it is essential for you to be sure that every item agreed upon between you and the landlord is stated in writing. This is particularly important when dealing with leases since many state laws provide that a long-term lease is an interest in land and can only be enforced if in writing.

The relationship between landlords and tenants is an ancient one that is undergoing a good deal of change. Care should be taken when examining a potential business location to determine exactly what you can do on the premises and whether the landlord or municipal rules will allow you to use the location for its intended purpose.

23

Pension Plans as Employee Benefits

One of the methods by which a business owner may attract and retain key personnel is to provide certain benefits. Today, one of the most important benefits for employees is the ability to participate in a pension plan.

A pension plan is a written savings program. If the plan meets the IRS's specific rules and regulations, then it is called a *qualified plan*, which means contributions are tax deductible to the person or the business making the investments. The earnings will grow, free of all taxes either to the plan sponsor or to the participants.

A qualified plan is one of the last remaining tax shelters available to highly compensated individuals. It may be used to set aside funds for retirement, and to attract and retain key employees. If properly structured and funded on a conservative basis with diversified portfolio investments, the plan should achieve financial security for the individual's retirement.

When choosing a plan, select the type that will most satisfactorily meet your needs and those of your employees.

There are essentially two types of qualified plans: defined contribution and defined benefit.

Defined Contribution Plans

In a defined contribution plan, the amount of money that is invested on behalf of the participant is "defined" as a percentage of his or her annual income. The amount of money that will be available to the participant at retirement is not defined. Interest and earnings on the investments made through the plan increase the retirement benefit for the individual plan participants. The longer the period of time over which investments are accumulated and interest is earned, the greater the amount of benefits that will be available to the participant at retirement.

Profit-sharing plans, salary savings or reduction plans such as 401(k)s, SIMPLE plans, and money purchase plans are all defined contribution plans, as are Simplified Employee Pension [Plans] (SEPs) and Employee Stock Ownership Plans (ESOPs).

Profit-Sharing Plans

If the revenue (income) from your business varies significantly from year to year, a profit-sharing plan may be the most appropriate type of plan to offer your employees. Contributions are determined at the end of the accounting year, which is usually December 31. Contributions to the plan can be determined annually by a vote of your business's management (i.e., managing partners or the board of directors), or by a formula previously designated in the plan's documents. Recent changes in federal laws no longer require business entities, such as corporations or certain types of LLCs, to declare a profit in order to make a contribution. Contributions to a profit-sharing plan are limited to a maximum of 25 percent of an employee's annual income and cannot exceed total contributions of $30,000 per year for each participant.

Salary Savings/Reduction Plans [also known as Thrift Plans]

These plans, which include 401(k)s, are a variant of profit-sharing plans. Under this type of plan, the employee elects to have a percentage of his or her gross salary diverted into a qualified plan. The employee's contributions are pretax dollars, so this type of plan provides the employee with significant tax savings. Depending on the plan, the employer may elect to match a portion of the contributions made by the employee. Usually the amount of the matching contribution has a limit.

The main feature of salary savings/reduction plans is that a portion of the cost shifts from the employer to the employee; the business, therefore, makes less of a cash contribution to this type of pension plan.

A major drawback is the limitation of contributions by highly compensated employees. The maximum contribution for 1996 and 1997 was $9,500. In addition, total contributions to the plan on behalf of the top one-third of highly compensated employees are dictated by the lower two-thirds of compensated employees, because employees must contribute the identical percentage of their incomes. If, therefore, the less highly compensated employees wish to contribute three percent of their incomes, the highly compensated employees may only contribute three percent of their incomes up to the statutory limit. Although there are exceptions, generally this plan is appropriate only in companies with at least twenty-five employees.

Simplified Employee Pension [Plans] [SEPs]

These plans are often viewed incorrectly as an alternative to the more highly structured qualified plans. The maximum contribution that the employer may contribute per participant to a SEP for 1997 is 15 percent of the compensation or $24,000, whichever is less. Contributions are based on an equal percentage of annual salary for all employees twenty-one years or older who have performed service for the employer during at least three out of five years and have received at least $400 (subject to cost of living adjustments). Although its low maintenance cost is an initial attraction, its simplicity results in a significant inflexibility that many employers are not willing to accept.

SAR/SEPs (Salary Reduction Simplified Employee Pension [Plans]) are no longer available after December 31, 1996. Existing SAR/SEPs are grandfathered in and are allowed to exist until the employer terminates them. A new salary reduction plan called the SIMPLE IRA was introduced to replace the SAR/SEP. This plan is available to employers with up to one hundred employees. Employees are eligible if they earned at least $5,000 during any of the previous two years and are expected to earn at least $5,000 during the current year. These requirements can be reduced or eliminated if the employer waives them. Maximum employee contribution is $6,000 per year. The employer is required to match up to 3 percent of the employee compensation. Vesting for the employer contributions is 100 percent and immediate.

Money Purchase Plans

Under this type of plan, the employee determines how much he or she wants to save each year. Although there are other restrictions, the primary parameters are: the lesser of 25 percent of annual income (20 percent of the gross earnings for the unincorporated business owner) or $30,000 in contributions per year per participant.

Employee Stock Ownership Plans [ESOPs]

In each of the defined contribution plans already discussed, the employee is specifically prohibited from owning more than 10 percent of the stock in the parent sponsor corporation as an asset of the plan. In an ESOP plan, the majority of the assets are shares of stock in the parent corporation. Generally, ESOPs are not useful for owners of small businesses.

Defined Benefit Plans

Contributions to a defined benefit plan are determined by a relatively complex formula, and then monitored by a professionally licensed enrolled actuary. Contributions to a defined benefit plan are not to exceed the lesser of 100 percent of the employee's annual average income for the three highest-salaried consecutive years or a specified amount, which is adjusted annually and dependent on changes in the Consumer Price Index (For 1997, $125,000 per worker). Excess earnings (investment income) greater than the assumptions made by the actuary (normally 8 percent) are used to reduce the cost of contributions to the plan by the employer.

Normally, defined benefit plans are appropriate where the business owner is "mature," with less than ten to fifteen working years until retirement. Defined benefit plans are appropriate—and potentially beneficial—for businesses that have enjoyed considerable financial success with limited fluctuations in cash flow. The defined benefit plan can be designed to drain excess funds and allocate them to retirement on behalf of the senior preferred participant (the principal owner). In many instances, this same advantage can be attained through the use of a target benefit plan.

Target Benefit Plans

The target benefit plan is receiving renewed interest as a result of changes in income tax law. This hybrid plan combines the contribution and benefit levels of a defined contribution plan with the recognition for senior (older) employees found in defined benefit plans.

As a result of changes under the Technical Corrections Act of 1987, a second addition to this hybrid category, known as an Age-Weighted Profit-Sharing Plan (AWPSP), has been developed. As with the target benefit plan, the contributions to this profit-sharing plan are "weighted," or skewed, toward senior employees.

Designing and Documenting a Plan

The creation of a qualified plan usually involves the creation and adoption of a trust agreement, disclosure of information for employees, and other pertinent language. As I mentioned earlier, plans must be in writing. Plans containing the standardized language preapproved by the IRS are available from several sources, including insurance companies, brokerage houses, and mutual fund companies. Each of these sources may have limitations, either in the language, investment opportunities, or requirements for the use of a third-party trustee, that should be carefully evaluated. It is, therefore, essential to work with an experienced professional when selecting and establishing a plan.

Since 1982, federal tax laws have been amended to allow unincorporated businesses the same status as corporations with regard to qualified pension plans. Further, this same legislation eliminated the need for a third-party administrator, thus allowing the employer to be the trustee (i.e, the care-taker) of his or her own plan.

Plans may be combined or "stacked" in order to more specifically meet the needs of the business; however, this creates the need for separate sets of rules and limitations. Stacking also increases the amount of administrative paperwork and forms, thus driving up the cost of operating and maintaining the plan.

The design features outlined below can be used to limit or reduce the cost of participation by employees in the employer-sponsored plan.

Testing

A key element of any qualified plan is to reward long-term service by employees. One method used to limit participation by employees who have been employed for a relatively short period of time is a vesting schedule. *Vesting* means 'having rights in,' which is to say that the employee has the right to all or part of the funds in the pension plan. Currently for small plans, the IRS recognizes two primary vesting formulas:

1. Five-year exclusion with 100 percent vesting (also known as "cliff" vesting, because it is all or nothing, like falling off a cliff). This formula does not allow vesting for employees with less than five years of service. Upon completion of five years of service, the employee is 100 percent vested in the plan.

2. Three- to seven-year graded vesting. This vesting formula can preclude participation by an employee until he or she has worked for at least one plan year. During years two and three, the employer is paying into the employee's account, but the employee has no rights to those funds. Following completion of the third plan year of employment, for the subsequent twelve months, the employee would be entitled to 20 percent of the funds that have been set aside for him or her. For each subsequent year of participation in the plan, the employee is vested an additional 20 percent. After completing seven years of plan participation, the employee is eligible to receive 100 percent of the contributions and interest earnings on the funds upon termination of employment.

Minimum Hours

The plan sponsor may limit the participation of employees by exempting those who work fewer than five hundred hours per year. This feature is very important for businesses that retain temporary employees.

Minimum Age

The plan sponsor may also limit participation of employees through the use of a minimum age requirement. Current law allows an employer to postpone participation by employees under twenty-one years of age. At the time the employee reaches age twenty-one, his or her total years of service must be applied to the vesting formula.

Integration

This feature allows the plan sponsor to recognize contributions made on behalf of the employee to Social Security. The plan sponsor applies two separate levels of contribution. The first is a minimum contribution that cannot exceed an employee's maximum contribution under Social Security. The second is on all income in excess of the first level. Current tax statutes limit the separation of the two levels of contributions to 7 percent.

Unions

Employees that are a part of a collective bargaining unit can be specifically exempted from participation in a qualified plan established by an employer.

Investments in a Qualified Plan

The primary governing factor regarding investments made by a qualified plan is contained in the Internal Revenue Code statement known as the "The Prudent Person Investment Principle." This means that investments should be made with primary consideration given to the preservation of salary or principal (amounts invested), and secondary consideration to growth and income.

Growth

In an investment, growth occurs when the original principal or amount invested increases in value—for example, shares of stock purchased at $1 per share increase in value to $1.25 per share.

Income

Income is derived through a principal investment that earns interest. Two of the most frequently asked questions are: What investments should I use in my pension plan? and How much should I invest in each one?

There are a plethora of investment opportunities, including stocks, bonds, money market accounts, real estate, and partnership interests. Therefore, it is essential that you confer with a qualified financial planner to structure your plan investments based on your goals, the economy, and other relevant factors.

24

Estate Planning

No matter what business you are involved with and no matter how successful you are in that business, the time that you will work with your business is limited by either retirement or death. Prudent businesspeople will make appropriate plans for both.

Proper estate planning will require the assistance of a knowledgeable lawyer and, perhaps, also a life insurance agent, an accountant, a real estate, art, or business appraiser, or a bank trust officer, depending on the nature and size of the estate. In this chapter we will consider the basic principles of estate planning. This discussion is not a substitute for the aid of a lawyer experienced in estate planning; rather, it is intended to introduce you to the basic principles, alert you to potential problems, and aid in preparing you to work with your estate planner(s).

The Will

A will is a legal instrument by which a person directs the distribution of property in his or her estate upon death. The maker of the will is called the *testator*. Gifts given by a will are referred to as *bequests* (personal property) or *devises* (real estate). Certain formalities are required by state law to create a valid will. About thirty states allow only formally witnessed wills, requiring that the instrument be in writing and signed by the testator, in the presence of two or more witnesses. The other states allow either witnessed or unwitnessed wills. If a will is entirely handwritten and signed by the testator, it is known as a *holographic* will.

A will is a unique document in two respects. First, if properly drafted it is *ambulatory*, meaning it can accommodate change, such as applying to property acquired after the will is made. Second, a will is *revocable*, meaning that the testator has the power to change or cancel it before death. Even if a testator makes a valid agreement not to revoke the will, the power to revoke it remains. If the testator uses that power, he or she may be liable for breach of contract.

Generally, courts do not consider a will to have been revoked unless it can be established that the testator either (1) performed a physical act of revocation, such as burning or tearing up a will, with intent to revoke it, or (2) later executed a valid will that revoked the previous will. Most state statutes also provide for automatic revocation of a will, in whole or in part, if the testator is subsequently divorced or married.

To change a will, the testator must execute a supplement, known as a *codicil*, which has the same formal requirements as those for creating a will. To the extent that the codicil contradicts the will, the contradicted parts of the will are revoked.

Payment of Testator's Debts

When the testator's estate is insufficient to satisfy all the bequests in the will after debts and taxes have been paid, some or all of the bequests in the will must be reduced or even eliminated entirely. The process of reducing or eliminating bequests is known as *abatement*, and the priorities for reduction are set according to the category of each bequest. The legally significant categories of gifts are generally as follows:

- *Specific* bequests or devises, meaning gifts of identifiable items ("I give to X all the furniture in my home")
- *Demonstrative* bequests or devises, meaning gifts that are to be paid out of a specified source unless that source contains insufficient funds, in which case the gifts will be paid out of the general assets ("I give to Y $1,000 to be paid from my shares of stock in ABC Corporation")
- *General* bequests, meaning gifts to be paid out of the general assets of an estate ("I give Z $1,000")
- *Residuary* bequests or devises, or gifts of whatever is left in the estate after all other gifts and expenses are satisfied ("I give the rest, residue, and remainder of my estate to Z").

Intestate property, or property not governed by a will but part of the testator's estate, is usually the first to be taken to satisfy claims against the estate. (If the will contains a valid residuary clause, there will be no such property.) Next, residuary bequests will be taken. If more money is needed, general bequests will be taken, and, lastly, specific and demonstrative bequests will be taken together in proportion to their value. Some states, however, provide that all gifts, regardless of type, abate proportionately.

Disposition of Property Not Willed

If the testator acquires more property during the time between signing the will and death, the disposition of such property will also be governed by the will, which, as previously noted, is ambulatory in nature. If such property falls within the description of an existing category in the will ("I give all my stock to X; I give all my real estate to Y"), it will pass along with all similar property. If it does not, and the will contains a valid residuary clause, such after-acquired property will go to the residuary legatees. If there is no residency clause, such property will pass outside the will to the persons specified in the state's law of intestate succession.

When a person dies without leaving a valid will, this is known as dying *intestate*. The estate of a person who dies intestate is distributed according to the state law of intestate succession, which specifies who is entitled to what parts of the estate. In general, intestate property passes to those persons having the nearest "degree of kinship" to the decedent. An intestate's surviving spouse will always receive a share, generally at least one-third of the estate. An intestate's surviving children generally get a share. If some of the children do not survive the intestate, the grandchildren of the intestate may be entitled to a share "by representation." *Representation* is a legal principle that means that if an heir does not survive the intestate, but has a child who does survive, that child will represent the nonsurviving heir and receive that parent's share in the estate. In other words, the surviving child stands in the shoes of a dead parent in order to inherit from a grandparent who dies intestate.

If there are no direct descendants surviving, the intestate's surviving spouse will take the entire estate or share it with the intestate's parents. If there is neither a surviving spouse nor any surviving direct descendant of the intestate, the estate will be distributed to the intestate's parents, or if the parents are not surviving, to the intestate's siblings by representation. If there are no surviving persons in any of these categories, the estate will go to surviving grandparents and their direct descendants. In this way, the family tree is constantly expanded in search of surviving relatives. If none of the persons specified in the law of intestate succession survive the testator, the intestate's property ultimately goes to the state. This is known as *escheat*. It should be noted that the laws of intestate succession make no provision for friends, in-laws, or stepchildren.

State law will often provide a testator's surviving spouse with certain benefits from the estate even if the spouse is left out of the testator's will. Historically, these benefits were known as *dower*, in the case of a surviving wife, or *curtesy*, in the case of a surviving husband. In place of the old dower and curtesy, modern statutes give the surviving spouse the right to "elect" against the will, and, thereby, receive a share equal to at least one-fourth of the estate. Here again, state laws vary; in some states, the surviving spouse's elective share is one-third. The historical concepts of dower and curtesy are in large part a result of the law's traditional recognition of an absolute duty on the part of the husband to provide for the wife. Modern laws are perhaps better justified by the notion that most property in a marriage should be shared because the financial success of either partner is due to the efforts of both.

Advantages to Having a Will

Now that we have some background as to what a will is and what happens without one, we can begin to look at some of the benefits of having a will. A will affords the opportunity to direct distribution of one's property and to set out limitations by making gifts conditional. For example, if an individual wishes to donate certain property to a specific charity, but only if certain conditions are adhered to, a will can make such conditions a prerequisite to the donation.

A will permits the testator to nominate an executor, called a "personal representative" in some states, to watch over the estate. If no executor is named in the will, the court will appoint one. A will permits the testator to give property to minors and to regulate the timing and uses of the property given (e.g., funds to be used exclusively for education). If the testator has unusual types of property, such as antiques, artworks, or publishable manuscripts, it is a good idea to appoint joint executors, one with financial expertise and the other with expertise in valuation in the field in question. If joint executors are used, some provision should be made in the will for resolving any deadlock between the two. For example, a neutral third party might be appointed as an arbitrator who is directed to resolve any impasses after hearing both sides. It is also advisable to define the scope of the executor's power by detailed instructions. A lawyer's help will be necessary to set forth all of these important considerations in legally enforceable, unambiguous terms. It is essential in a will to avoid careless language that might be subject to attack by survivors unhappy with the will's provisions. A lawyer's assistance is also crucial to avoid making bequests that are not legally enforceable because they are contrary to public policy (e.g., if an individual gets married, the bequest will fail).

In addition to giving the testator significant posthumous control over division of property, a carefully drafted will can greatly reduce the overall amount of estate tax paid at death. The following information on taxing structures relates to federal estate taxation. State estate taxes often contain similar provisions, but state law must always be consulted for specifics.

The Gross Estate

The first step in evaluating an estate for tax purposes is to determine the so-called gross estate. The *gross estate* will include all property over which the deceased had significant control at the time of death. In addition to certain bank accounts, examples would include properly held residences, investments that have been structured to avoid probate, certain life insurance proceeds and annuities, jointly held interests, and revocable transfers.

Under current tax laws, the executor of an estate may elect to value the property in the estate either as of the date of death or as of a date six months after death. The estate property must be valued in its entirety at the time chosen. However, if the executor elects to value the estate six months after death and certain pieces of property are distributed or sold before then, that property will be valued as of the date of distribution or sale.

Fair market value is defined as the price at which property would change hands between a willing buyer and a willing seller when both buyer and seller have reasonable knowledge of all relevant facts. Such a determination is often very difficult to make, especially when items such as artwork are involved. Although the initial determination of fair market value is generally made by the executor when the estate tax return is filed, the Internal Revenue Service may disagree with the executor's valuation and assign assets a much higher fair market value. For example, in 1979 the IRS claimed that Jacqueline Susann's diary had an estate tax value of $3,800,000 as a literary property. The diary, which neither Susann nor her executor had considered particularly valuable, had been destroyed by the executor pursuant to Susann's directions.

When an executor and the Internal Revenue Service disagree with regard to valuation, the court will decide the matter. In most cases, the burden will be on the taxpayer to prove the value of the asset. Thus, expert testimony and evidence of the sale of the same or similar properties will be helpful, as in cases involving original manuscripts and drawings. In general, courts are reluctant to determine valuation by formula.

Generally, estate taxes must be paid when the estate tax return is filed (within nine months of the date of death), although arrangements may be made to spread payments out over a number of years if necessary. It is not uncommon for executors to be forced to sell properties for less than full value in order to pay taxes. This can be avoided by obtaining insurance policies, the proceeds of which can be set up in a trust. (For an explanation of a trust, see below.)

The law allows a number of deductions from the gross estate in determining the amount of the taxable estate. The taxable estate is the basis upon which the tax owing is computed. The following section gives you a closer look at some of the key deductions used to arrive at the amount of the taxable estate.

The Taxable Estate

Figuring the taxable estate is the second major step in evaluating an estate for tax purposes, after determining the gross estate. Typical deductions from the gross estate include funeral expenses, certain estate administration expenses, debts and enforceable claims against the estate, mortgages and liens, and, perhaps most significant, the marital deduction and the charitable deduction.

The marital deduction allows the total value of any interest in property that passes from the decedent to the surviving spouse to be subtracted from the value of the gross estate. The government will eventually get its tax on this property, when the spouse dies, but only to the extent such interest is included in the spouse's gross estate. The spouse, of course, may limit or eliminate the estate tax on his or her estate by implementing certain estate-planning procedures. This deduction may occur even in the absence of a will making a gift to the surviving spouse, since state law generally provides that the spouse is entitled to at least one-fourth of the overall estate regardless of the provisions of the will.

The charitable deduction refers to the tax deduction allowed upon the transfer of property from an estate to a recognized charity. Since the definition of a charity for tax purposes is quite technical, it is advisable to insert a clause in the will providing that if the institution specified to receive the donation does not qualify for the charitable deduction, the bequest shall go to a substitute qualified institution at the choice of the executor.

Once deductions are figured, the taxable estate is taxed at the rate specified by the Unified Estate and Gift Tax Schedule. The unified tax imposes the same rate of tax on gifts made by will as on gifts made during life. It is a progressive tax, meaning the percent paid in taxes increases with the amount of property involved. The rates rise significantly for larger estates, for example, from 18 percent, where the cumulative total of taxable estate and taxable gifts is under $10,000, to 55 percent, where the cumulative total is over $3,000,000. Federal estate tax is also reduced by state death tax credit or actual state death tax, whichever is less. Tax credits result in a $600,000 exemption, which is available to every estate. Over the next ten years, the $600,000 exemption will increase to $625,000 in 1998 and to $1,000,000 by 2006. There will also be an additional exemption for families with qualifying businesses or farms, allowing a total exemption of $1.3 million. These exemptions, combined with the unlimited marital deduction, allow most estates to escape estate taxes altogether.

Distributing Property Outside the Will

Property can be distributed outside the will by making *inter vivos* gifts (given during the giver's lifetime), either outright or by placing the property in trust prior to death. A potential advantage to distributing property outside the will is that the property escapes the delays and expense of *probate*, the court procedure by which a will is validated and administered. It used to be that there were also significant tax advantages to making inter vivos gifts rather than making gifts by will, but since the estate and gift tax rates are now unified, there are few remaining tax advantages. One remaining advantage to making an inter vivos gift is that if the gift appreciates in value between the time the gift is made and death, the appreciated value will not be subject to estate tax. If the gift were made by will, the added value would be taxable since the gift would be valued on the estate tax return as of date of death (or six months after). This value difference can represent significant tax savings for the heirs of someone whose business suddenly becomes successful and rapidly increases in value.

The other advantage to making an inter vivos gift involves the yearly exclusion. A yearly exclusion of $10,000 per recipient is available on inter vivos gifts. For example, if $15,000 worth of gifts were given to an individual in one year, only $5,000 worth of gifts will actually be taxable to the donor who is responsible for the gift tax. A married couple can combine their gifts and claim a yearly exclusion of $20,000 per recipient. The yearly exclusion will be adjusted for inflation (in $1,000 increments) starting in 1999. Gifts made within three years of death used to be included in the gross estate on the theory that they were made in contemplation of death. Recent amendments to the tax laws, however, have done away with the three-year rule for most purposes. The three-year rule is still applicable to gifts of life insurance and to certain transfers involving stock redemption or tax liens; the rule also applies to certain valuation schemes, the details of which are too complex to discuss here.

The donor must file gift tax returns for any year in which gifts made exceeded $10,000 to any one donee. It is not necessary to file returns when a gift to any one donee amounts to less than $10,000. However, where it is possible that valuation of the gift will become an issue with the IRS, it may be a good idea to file a return anyway. Filing the return starts the three-year statute of limitations running. Once the statute of limitations period has expired, the IRS will be barred from filing suit for unpaid taxes or for tax deficiencies due to higher government valuations of the gifts. If a taxpayer omits includable gifts amounting to more than 25 percent of the total amount of gifts stated in the return, the statute of limitations is extended to six years. There is no statute of limitations for fraudulent returns filed with the intent to evade tax.

In order to qualify as an inter vivos, or living, gift for tax purposes, a gift must be complete and final. Control is an important issue. If a giver retains the right to revoke a gift, the gift may be found to be testamentary in nature, even if the right to revoke was never exercised (unless the gift was made in trust). The gift must also be delivered. An actual, physical delivery is best, but a symbolic delivery may suffice if there is strong evidence of intent to make an irrevocable gift. An example of symbolic delivery is when the donor puts something in a safe and gives the intended recipient the only key.

Another common way to transfer property outside the will is to place the property in a trust that is created prior to death. A *trust* is simply a legal arrangement by which one person holds certain property for the benefit of another. The person holding the property is the *trustee*; those for whose benefit it is held are the *beneficiaries*. To create a valid trust, the giver must identify the trust property, make a declaration of intent to create the trust, transfer property to the trust, and name identifiable beneficiaries. If no trustee is named, a court will appoint one. The *settlor*, or creator of the trust, may also be designated as trustee, in which case segregation of the trust property satisfies the delivery requirement. Trusts can be created by will, in which case they are termed *testamentary* trusts, but these trust properties will be probated along with the rest of the will. To avoid probate, the settlor must create a valid inter vivos trust.

Generally, in order to qualify as an inter vivos trust, a valid interest in property must be transferred before the death of the creator of the trust. If the settlor fails to name a beneficiary for the trust or to make delivery of the property to the trustee before death, the trust will likely be termed testamentary. Such a trust will be deemed invalid unless the formalities required for creating a will were complied with.

A trust will not be termed testamentary simply because the settlor retained significant control over the trust, such as the power to revoke or modify the trust. For example, when a person makes a deposit in a savings account in his or her own name as trustee for another, and reserves the power to withdraw the money or to revoke the trust, the trust will be enforceable by the beneficiary upon the death of the depositor, providing the depositor has not in fact revoked the trust. Many states allow the same type of arrangement in authorizing joint bank accounts with rights of survivorship as valid will substitutes. Property transferred under one of these arrangements is thus passed outside the will and need not go through probate. However, even though such an arrangement escapes probate, the trust property will probably be counted as part of the gross estate for tax purposes because the settlor retained significant control. In addition, if the deceased settlor created a revocable trust for the purpose of decreasing the share of a surviving spouse, in some states the trust will be declared illusory—in effect, invalid. The surviving spouse is then granted the legal share not only from the probated estate but from the revocable trust.

Life insurance trusts can be used for paying estate taxes. The proceeds will not be taxed if the life insurance trust is irrevocable and the beneficiary is someone other than the estate, such as a friend or relative in an individual capacity or the business. This is especially important for businesspeople, since without a life insurance trust, their survivors might be forced to sell estate assets for less than their real value in order to pay estate taxes.

Probate

Briefly described, *probate* is the legal process by which a decedent's estate is administered in a systemic and orderly manner, and with finality. The laws that govern the probate process vary among the states. One of the principal functions of probate administration is to provide a means to transfer ownership of a decedent's probate property. Accordingly, probate administration occurs without regard to whether the decedent died testate (with a will) or intestate (without a will).

In the course of probate administration, the following occurs:

1. A decedent's will is admitted to probate as the decedent's "last" will
2. Someone (sometimes referred to as the *personal representative, executor,* or *administrator*) is appointed by the court to take charge of the decedent's property and financial affairs
3. Interested persons are notified of the commencement of probate administration
4. Information concerning the decedent's estate is gathered
5. Probate property is assembled and preserved
6. Debts and taxes are determined, paid and/or challenged
7. Claims against the decedent's estate are paid and/or challenged
8. Conflicting claims of entitlement to the decedent's property are disposed of
9. At the conclusion of the process, remaining estate property is distributed to the appropriate persons or entities

While probate administration is pending, distributions of the decedent's property are suspended to allow creditors, claimants, devisees, and heirs the opportunity to protect their respective rights.

Probate property consists of the decedent's solely owned property as of the date of death. Property jointly held by the decedent and another person with the right of survivorship (e.g., a residence owned jointly by a married couple, or stock certificates held jointly with right of survivorship) passes to the survivor and is not a part of the decedent's probate estate. Likewise, the proceeds of life insurance on the decedent's life is not part of the probate estate (unless the estate is the designated beneficiary). It is, therefore, possible for a wealthy individual to die leaving little or no probate property.

Conclusion

All businesspeople should give some thought to estate planning and take the time to execute a will. Without a will, there is simply no way to control the disposition of one's property. Sound estate planning may include transfers outside of the will since these types of arrangements escape the delays and expenses of probate. Certain types of trusts can be valuable will substitutes, but they may be subject to challenge by a surviving spouse. Since successful estate planning is complex, it is essential to work with a lawyer skilled in this field.

25

How to Find a Lawyer and Accountant

Most business people expect to seek the advice of a lawyer only occasionally, for counseling on important matters such as the decision to incorporate or the purchase of a building. If this is your concept of the attorney's role in your business, I recommend that you reevaluate it. Most small businesses would operate more efficiently and more profitably in the long run if they had a relationship with a business attorney more like that between a family doctor and his patient, i.e., an ongoing relationship that allows the attorney to get to know the business well enough to engage in preventive legal counseling and to assist in planning, thus making possible the solution of many problems before they occur.

If your business is small or undercapitalized, you are doubtless anxious to keep operating costs down. You probably do not relish the idea of paying an attorney to get to know your business if you are not involved in an immediate crisis. However, it is a good bet that a visit with a competent business lawyer right now will result in the raising of issues vital to the future of your business. There is good reason why larger, successful businesses employ one or more attorneys full time as in-house counsel. Ready access to legal advice is something you should not deny your business at any time, for any reason.

An attorney experienced in business law can give you important information regarding the risks unique to your business. Furthermore, a lawyer can advise you regarding your rights and obligations in your relationship with present and future employees, the rules that apply in your state regarding the hiring and firing of employees, permissible collection practices, and so forth. Ignorance of these issues and violation of the rules can result in financially devastating lawsuits and even criminal penalties. Since each state has its own laws covering certain business practices, state laws must be consulted on many areas covered in this book. A competent local business attorney is, therefore, your best source of information on many issues that will arise in the running of your business.

What is really behind all the hoopla about preventive legal counseling? Are lawyers simply seeking more work? Admittedly, as businesspeople, lawyers want business. But what you should consider is economic reality: *Most legal problems cost more to solve or defend after they arise than it would have cost to prevent their occurrence in the first place.* Litigation is notoriously inefficient and expensive. You do not want to sue or to be sued, if you can help it. The expense is shocking; for instance, it can cost close to $100 per day simply to use a courtroom for trial. Pretrial procedures run into the thousands of dollars in most cases. The cost of defending a case filed against you or your business is something you have no choice but to incur, unless you choose to default, which is almost never advisable.

The lawyer who will be most valuable to your young business will likely not be a Raymond Burr or Robert Redford character, but rather a meticulous person who does most of his or her work in an office, going over your business forms, your employee contracts, or your corporate bylaws. This person should have a good reputation in the legal community as well as in the business community. You might pay over $100 per hour for the attorney, but if the firm has a good reputation, it likely employs a well-trained pro-fessional staff that can reduce the amount of attorney time required.

One of the first items you should discuss with your lawyer is the fee structure. You are entitled to an estimate, though unless you enter into an agreement to the contrary with the attorney, the estimate is just that. Business lawyers generally charge by the hour, though you may be quoted a flat rate for a specific service such as incorporation or registering your trademark.

Finding a Lawyer

If you do not know any attorneys, ask other businesspeople if they know any good ones. You want either a lawyer who specializes in business, or a general practitioner who has many satisfied business clients. Finding the lawyer who is right for you is like finding the right doctor: you may have to shop around a bit. Your city, county, and state bar associations may have helpful referral services. A good tip is to find out who is in the business law section of the state or county bar association, or who has served on special bar committees dealing with law reform. It may also be useful to find out if any articles covering the area of law with which you are concerned have been published in either scholarly journals or continuing-legal-education publications, and if the author is available to assist you. It is a good idea to hire a specialist or law firm with a number of specialists rather than a general practitioner. While it is true that you may pay more per hour for the expert, still, you will not have to fund his learning time, and experience is valuable. In this regard, you may wish to keep in mind that it is uncommon for a lawyer to specialize in business practice and also handle criminal matters. Thus, if you are faced with a criminal prosecution for the death of an employee as discussed in chapter 16, then you should be searching for an experienced criminal defense lawyer.

One method by which you can attempt to evaluate an attorney in regard to representing business clients is by consulting the *Martindale-Hubbell Law Directory* in your local county law library. While this may be useful, the mere fact that an attorney's name does not appear in the book should not be given too much weight, since there is a charge for being included and some lawyers may have chosen not to pay for the listing. You may also wish to search the

World Wide Web. Many attorneys have established Web sites, and the better sites usually include extensive résumés on the firm, as well as the areas of law in which it has expertise.

After you have obtained several recommendations for attorneys, it is appropriate for you to talk with them for a short period of time to determine whether you would be comfortable working with them. Do not be afraid to ask about their background experience, and whether they feel they can help you.

Once you have completed the interview process, select the person who appears to satisfy your needs. The rest is up to you. Contact your lawyer whenever you believe a legal question has arisen. Your attorney should aid you in identifying which questions require legal action or advice and which require business decisions. Generally, lawyers will deal only with legal issues, though they may help you to evaluate business problems.

I encourage my clients to feel comfortable about calling me at the office during the day or at home in the evening. Some lawyers, however, may resent having their personal time invaded. Some, in fact, do not list their home telephone numbers. You should learn your attorney's preference early on.

The attorney-client relationship is such that you should feel comfortable when confiding in your attorney. This person will not disclose your confidential communications; in fact, a violation of this rule, depending on the circumstances, can be considered an ethical breach that could subject the attorney to professional sanctions.

If you take the time to develop a good working relationship with your attorney, it may well prove to be one of your more valuable business assets.

Finding an Accountant

In addition to an attorney, most small businesses will need the services of a competent accountant to aid with tax planning, the filing of periodic reports, and annual tax returns. Finding a CPA with whom your business is compatible is similar to finding an attorney. You should ask around and learn which accountants are servicing businesses similar to yours. State professional accounting associations may also provide a referral service or point you to a directory of accountants in your region. You should interview prospective accountants to determine whether you feel you can work with them and whether you feel their skills will be compatible with your business needs.

Like your attorney, your accountant can provide valuable assistance in planning for the future of your business. It is important to work with professionals you trust and with whom you are able to relate on a professional level.

Index

Accounts receivable
  as collateral, 39
advertising, 129–134
  celebrities' rights of
    publicity, 131
  celebrity endorsements, 131
  comparative, 130–131
  consumer protection laws,
    129
  geographic locations, 132–
    133
  government regulations,
    129–130
  misleading, 129
  trade dress, 133
  World Wide Web, 140–141
Age-Weighted Profit-Sharing
  Plan (AWPSP), 217
  See also pension plan
Allen v. Commissioner, 190
America's Research Group, 135–
  136
American Geophysical Union v.
  Texaco, Inc., 120
American Registry for Internet
  Numbers, 138
Americans with Disabilities Act
  of 1990, 209
arbitrator, 18
articles of incorporation, 9
Ashton-Tate Corp. v. Ross, 112
attorney. See lawyer

Baie v. Commissioner, 193
bankruptcy, 9, 45
  discharging debt, 76
  individual (Chapter 13), 77
  of consignee, 65–67
  of franchise, 81
  reorganization (Chapter 11),
    76–77
  straight, 76
Berne Convention, 108
board of directors, 9
  removing a member, 9
  voting deadlock, 21
borrowing capital, 29–46
  application, 43–44
  proposal, 30–31
  repayment terms, 41, 45
  See also loan
Buchwald v. Paramount
  Studios, 126
business name, 16

business plan, 23–27
business potential, 33
business tax year, 22
business-expense deductions, 189–202
    capital expenditures, 196–197
    charitable, 200–201
    current expenses, 196
    depreciation of capital expenditures,
        196
    disability, 197
    entertainment, 198–200
    health insurance, 202
    IRS scrutiny, 199–200
    logbook of, 200
    office-at-home, 191–196
    Social Security, 197
    travel, 197–200
    withholding-tax, 197
    See also tax
buy-sell agreement, 20–21
    See also securities

Capitalization, 21
C corporation, 11, 12, 188
Cardozo, Benjamin, 156–156, 158
cash discounts, 73
caveat emptor, 156
caveat vendor, 156
certified public accountant (CPA), 15–16,
        236–237
Child Protection Act of 1966, 159
Child Protection and Toy Safety act of
        1969, 159
Church of Scientology, 137
collapsible corporation, 189
collateral, 31, 36, 38–408
collections, 69–77
    lawsuits, 74
    small claims court, 74–75
collective works, 114
collection agency, 73–74
co-maker, 38
Commerce, U.S. Department of, 80
Commissioner of Patents and Trademarks,
        127
common law trademark, 96, 98
Communications Decency Act, 141–143
Community for Creative Non-Violence v.
        Reid, 113
confidentiality and nondisclosure

    agreement, 91
consignment, 63–68, 72
    advantages and disadvantages of, 63–64
    art-consignment legislation, 67–68
    artist-dealer laws, 66–67
    sign laws, 65
Consumer Price Index, 216
Consumer Product Safety Act, 160
consumer protection laws, 145–153, 159–
        160
    breach of warranty, 151
    Child Protection Act, 159
    Child Protection and Toy Safety Act of
        1969, 159
    Consumer Product Safety Act, 160
    cooling-off period, 151–152
    Flammable Fabrics Act, 160
    Hazardous Substance Labeling Act, 159
    mail-order sales, 152
contracts, 53–62
    acceptance of, 55–56
    breach of, 53
    consideration of, 55–56
    elements of, 53
    express, 54
    implied, 54–57
    no-cost written agreement, 59
    offer, 55–56
    oral, 54
    written, 54, 58–59
    written confirmation, 59
co-op insurance fund, 172
copyrights, 107–121
    Constitutional rights, 108
    exempted use, 119–121
    fair use, 119–121
    notice requirement, 115
    ownership of, 111–114
    period of protection, 117
    registering, 116–118
Copyright Act of 1909, 114, 115
copyright infringement, 118–119
    innocent infringer, 116
    statute of limitations, 118
Copyright Office, 127
Copyright Revision Act of 1976, 108, 110–
        111, 115, 116
corporate debentures, 10
corporate bonds, 10
corporate notes, 10

corporate reinvestment, 10
corporation, 7–12
    articles of incorporation, 9
    business structure of, 19–22
    bylaws, 9, 20
    distribution of earnings, 11
    employee benefits, 10, 22
    income, 10
    liability shield, 8
    perpetual existence, 8
    tax advantages, 187
    taxation, 7
    transfer of ownership, 8
counterfeit currency, 70
covenants, 43
credit card fraud, 70
creditworthiness, 30, 31–32, 37
cyberspace, 135–144

Debt burden, 45
debt-equity ratio, 37, 48
Deering v. Blair, 190
defined benefit plan, 214
    See also pension plan
defined contribution plan, 214
    See also pension plan
derivative works, 113–114
distress sale, 36, 44
dividends, 189
    See also stock
double taxation, 10–11, 188

Earnings projections, 51
e-mail, 144
employee, 175–182
    benefits, 178, 213–220
    probationary period, 182
    progressive discipline, 182
    termination of 180–182
    whistle-blowing, 181
    wrongful termination, 180–182
Employee Stock Ownership Plans
        (ESOPs), 214, 216
employment contracts, 175–177
    components of, 175–177
    contractual rights, 182
    disclosure of hazardous conditions, 180
    termination of, 177
encryption, 143–144
    See also World Wide Web

endorser, 38
Engdahl v. Commissioner, 191
equity financing, 51
estate planning, 221–232, 227
    distributing property outside of will,
        228–231
    federal estate tax, 228
    gross estate, 226–227
    inter vivos trusts, 228–230
    marital deduction, 228
    probate, 228, 231–232
    right of survivorship, 230, 231–232
    state death tax credit, 228
    taxable estate, 227–228
    testamentary trusts, 230
    three-year rule, 229
    trusts, 228, 229–230
    Unified Estate and Gift Tax Schedule,
        228
    will, 222–225
European Patent Regime, 88
exclusivity agreements, 26
expense accounts, 17

Fair Labor Standards Act, 206
family partnership, 186
Federal Art Hazard Bill, 179
federal tax ID number, 22
Federal Trade Commission (FTC), 80, 83–
        84, 130, 140–141, 160
field warehousing, 40
financial data, 33, 51
    balance sheet, 33
    profit and loss statement, 33
financial problems, 34
firewall, 143
fixed assets, 32
Flammable Fabrics Act, 160
Food and Drug Administration, 130
foreclosure, 44
franchise, 38, 79–83
    bankruptcy of, 81
    financial statements, 81
    statistical information, 81
    territorial limitations, 81
    training programs, 81
Franchise Opportunity Handbook, 80

Goods, definition of, 58
guarantor's promise to pay, 38

Harassment, 144
Hazardous Substance Labeling Act, 159
hazards in the workplace, 178–180
   hazardous substances, 179
   toxic materials, 179
home office deduction, 191–196
   allocable portion, 194
   allowable depreciation, 195
   nonrecognition of gain, 195
   See also tax

Income spreading, 184
   among family members, 185–186
   deferred payments, 184–185
   installments, 184
   negotiable note, 184
incorporating a family, 186
independent contractors, 173–175
industrywide standards, 159
initial public offering, 49–50
insurance, 164–172
   business, 163–172
   co-op fund, 172
   for partnerships, 4
   insurable interest, 165
   key-person, 21
   law, 165–166
   leased property, 210
   liability, 3, 141
   Lloyd's of London, 163–164
   overinsuring, 169
   premiums, 165
   product liability, 153, 160–161
   reforming a policy, 168
   risk, 166
   risk-spreading, 166
   scheduled property, 171
   tax deduction of premium, 172
   underinsuring, 169–170
   underwriting, 164
   unemployment, 177
   unscheduled property, 169
   unvalued policy, 166
   valued policy, 166
intellectual property, 126–127
   acknowledgment of owner, 126–127
   as collateral, 40
   employee use, 176
   on World Wide Web, 137–140
interest on overdue payments, 73

Internal Revenue Code, 184, 186, 188, 194
Internal Revenue Service, 184, 186, 188,
   191,192, 196, 217, 226, 229
International Ladies Garment Workers
   Union, 206
Internet access provider, 137
inventory, as collateral, 40
invoicing, 72
IRA, 3
   for sole proprietors, 3
   See also pension plan

Labor unions, 206
Lanham Act of 1946, 97, 98, 100, 102–104,
   134
lawyers, 233–236
   attorney-client relationship, 236
   ethical breach, 236
   in-house council, 234
   litigation, 234
lease, assignment of, 38
lease, commercial, 207–211
   insurance, 210
   long-term, 208
   restrictions, 208
   security, 210–211
   short-term, 208
   zoning, 210–211
letters patent, 89
liability, 155–161
   absolute, 67
   design defects, 158
   federal law, 159–160
   product, 156–161
   shield from, 8, 12, 19, 187
   strict liability, 158
licensing, 123–127
   trademark, 123–127
   business, 178
life insurance policies, as collateral, 39
limited partnership, 5–7
limited liability company (LLC), 12
   business structure of, 19–22
   certificate of participation, 20
   employee benefits, 22
   family-owned, 186
   tax advantages, 187
limited liability partnership (LLP),12–13
   business structure of, 19–22
   certificate of participation, 20

employee benefits, 22
liquidation, 45
loan, 29–46
    application, 43–44
    proposal, 30–31
    repayment terms, 41, 45

Magnuson-Moss Warranty Act, 150
mail-order sales, 152
Mandel v. Pikowsky, 205
market expansion, 79–86
market research, 25
Martindale-Hubbell Law Directory, 236
Maxtone-Graham v. Burtchaell, 120
Meiers v. Commissioner, 193
merchant, definition of, 59, 147
Meta Consulting Group, 135
minority owners, 13
Moller v. United States, 194
money purchase plan, 216
multilevel marketing, 83–86
    buyback policy, 85
    distributor activity, 85
    earnings statements, 85
    inventory requirement, 85
    investment requirement, 85
    protective regulations, 84
    sales commission, 85

Negligence, in a partnership, 3
net earning power, 41
net worth, 48
Netscape Communications, 140
Network Solutions, 138
Nimmer, Professor Melville, 111
no-cost written agreements, 59
    See also contracts
noncompetition agreements, 176
nonprofit corporation, 11
Notice of Allowance, 99
*Novosel v. Nationwide Insurance
    Company*, 181

Occupational Safety and Health
    Administration, 179
Official Gazette, 98–99

Partnership, 3–7
    business structure of, 16
    death of partner, 6
    dissolution of, 4, 19
    division of profits, 4
    liabilities, 7
    losses of, 4
    management structure of, 4
    prohibited acts, 18
    recapitalization of, 19
    reorganization of, 19
    retirement of partner, 6
    taxes, 5, 188
    unintended, 7
    voting deadlock, 18
partnership agreement, 4, 16–19
Patent and Trademark Office (PTO), 94,
    98–102
patents, 87–92
    design patents, 88
    international patents, 88
    licensing, 125
    mechanical patents, 88
pension plan, 213–220
    Age-Weighted Profit-Sharing Plan
        (AWPSP), 217
    defined benefit, 214, 216–217
    defined contribution, 214
    designing and documenting, 217–220
    Employee Stock Ownership Plans
        (ESOPs), 214, 216
    for sole proprietors, 3
    growth of, 220
    income from, 220
    integration, 219
    investments in, 219
    money purchase plans, 216
    qualified plan, 213
    salary savings and reduction plans,
        214–215
    SIMPLE IRA, 214, 215–216
    Simplified Employee Pension [Plans]
        (SEPs), 214, 215–216
    target benefit plans, 217
    testing, 218
    unions, 219
periodic reporting, 42
personal checks, 71–72
personal holding company, 188
Playboy magazine, 142
point-of-sale payments, 70
Principal Register, 97, 100–102
privatizing, 52

profits, of partnership, 4
profit motive, 189
profit-sharing plans, 214
publication, 108
pyramid schemes, 83

R eal estate holdings, as collateral, 39
Register of Copyrights, 116
Reno v. ACLU, 142
repayment ability, 33
retailers, 57
royalties, 188

S corporation, 11–12,
    distributable profits, 12
    distributable losses, 12
    taxes on, 11–12, 188
salary savings and reduction plans, 214–
    215
savings accounts, as collateral, 39
Securities and Exchange Commission
    (SEC), 50–51, 52
securities, 47–52
    disadvantages of, 49
    laws, 50
    registration, 48
    securities compliance exemption, 48
    selling agent, 51–52
    underwriter, 51–52
    See also stock
security interests, as collateral, 39
server protection, 143–144
shareholders
    common, 9
    distribution to, 188
    preferred, 9
SIMPLE IRA, 214, 215–216
    See also pension plan
Simplified Employee Pension [Plans]
    (SEPs), 214, 215–216
    See also pension plan
SIPO Performances and Phonograms
    Treaty, 143
Social Security Administration, 136
Social Security withholding, 177
sole proprietorship, 2–3, 188
Soliman v. Commissioner, 193
Small Business Administration, 25
spam, 144
Statute of Frauds, 58, 60, 61

Stevens, Justice John Paul, 142
stock, 40, 47–52
    as collateral, 40
    common, 9
    dividend preference, 9
    initial public offering, 49–50
    issuing, 48
    preferred, 9
    sale of, 189
    underwriting, 51–52
    See also securities
sublicense, 125
suppliers, 26, 57
Supplemental Register, 98, 100

T arget benefit plans, 217
tax, 183–202
    accumulated-earnings, 188
    capital gains, 173, 184
    capital interest, 186
    deductions, 161, 172, 185, 188, 189–
        202
    grants, prizes, and awards, 201–202
    fixed-rate system, 172
    income, 19
    marginal rate, 186
    municipal, 178
    passive investment income, 188
    payroll, 3, 187
    personal exemption, 185
    personal-dependency exemption, 185
    planning, 183
    rate, 183
    regular corporate, 188
    self-employment, 194–195
    standard deduction, 185
    unemployment, 187
    withholding, 177
Tax Reform Act of 1986, 187, 201
Taxpayer Relief Act of 1997, 184, 193, 195
Technical Corrections Act of 1987, 217
Total News, Inc., 140
trade dress, 133–134
trade secrets, 87–92, 143
    protection, 89–92
trade shows, 25
trade usage, 148
trademark, 93–105
    antidilution, 103–104
    common law, 96, 98

infringement, 102–103, 138–140
intent-to-use application, 94
loss, 102–103
registration of, 97–102, 104
unauthorized use, 132
Trademark Law Revision Act of 1988, 97–99
Trademark Office, 82
trade-name infringement, 16
Treasury regulations, 189
Truth-in-Lending Act, 73
Two Pesos v. Taco Cabana, 133

Undercapitalization, 37
underwriting, 51–52
   best efforts, 52
   firm, 51
   standby, 51–52
Unified Estate and Gift Tax Schedule, 228
Uniform Commercial Code (UCC), 56–57, 59, 65–67, 145, 147
Uniform Offering Circular, 80–82
union requirements, 178
United States Department of Labor, 205–206
Universal Studios, et al. v. Sony Corporation, et. al., 119

Vanderbilt, Reginald, 190
venture capital, 23

Wage and hour laws, 178
warehouse receipts, as collateral, 39
warranties, 145–153
   breach of, 151
   disclaimers, 149–151
   express, 145–147
   full, 150
   implied, 147–149
   limited, 151
   of merchantability, 147, 149–150
   of title, 148, 150
   against infringement, 148–149
will, 222–226
   abatement, 222
   ambulatory, 222, 223
   bequests, 222, 225
   breach of contract, 222
   charitable deduction, 227
   codicil, 222

curtesy, 224
devises, 222
dower, 224
escheat, 224
executor, 225, 231
fair market value, 226
gross estate, 226–227
heir, 224
holographic, 222
interstate property, 223
intestate, 223, 231
legatee, 223
marital deduction, 227
probate, 226, 228, 231–232
representation, 224
residuary bequests, 223
residuary clause, 223
revocable, 222
rights of survivorship, 230, 231–232
taxable estate, 227–228
testate, 231
testator, 222, 225
See also estate planning
worker's compensation, 177
works for hire, 112–113
workspace deduction, 191
World Intellectual Property Organization, 143
   WIPO Treaty of 1996, 143
World Wide Web, 124, 136–144, 236
wrongful termination, 180–182

Zoning for work at home, 203–206
   business license, 204
   federal regulations, 205–206
   home-occupation permit, 204
   local restrictions, 203–205
   rent-stabilization laws, 205

Books from Allworth Press

The Law (In Plain English)® for Photographers *by Leonard DuBoff*
(softcover, 6 × 9, 208 pages, $18.95)

Legal-Wise: Self-Help Legal Guide for Everyone, Third Edition
by Carl W. Battle, Attorney-at-Law (softcover, 8½ × 11, 208 pages, $18.95)

Hers: The Wise Woman's Guide to Starting a Business on $2,000 or Less,
Revised Edition *by Carol Milano* (softcover, 6 × 9, 224 pages, $16.95)

**The Retirement Handbook: How to Maximize Your Assets and Protect Your Quality
of Life** *by Carl W. Battle, Attorney-at-Law* (softcover, 6 × 9, 256 pages, $18.95)

**The Patent Guide: A Friendly Handbook for Protecting and Profiting from
Patents** *by Carl W. Battle, Attorney-at-Law* (softcover, 6 × 9, 192 pages, $18.95)

**The Copyright Guide: A Friendly Handbook for Protecting and Profiting from
Copyrights** *by Lee Wilson, Attorney-at-Law* (softcover, 6 × 9, 192 pages, $18.95)

**The Trademark Guide: A Friendly Handbook for Protecting and Profiting from
Trademarks** *by Lee Wilson, Attorney-at-Law* (softcover, 6 × 9, 192 pages, $18.95)

Old Money: The Mythology of Welath in America *by Tad Crawford*
(softcover, 6 × 9, 340 pages, $16.95)

Once in Golconda: A True Drama of Wall Street 1920–1938 *by John Brooks*
Introduction *by Tad Crawford* (hardcover, 5½ × 8½, 320 pages, $21.95)

The Go-Go Years: The Drama and Crashing Finale of Wall Street's Bullish 60s
by John Brooks (hardcover, 6¾ × 9½, 392 pages, $24.95)

Immigration Questions and Answers, Revised Edition
by Carl R. Baldwin, Attorney-at-Law (softcover, 6 × 9, 176 pages, $14.95)

**Your Living Trust and Estate Plan: How to Maximize Your Family's Assets and
Protect Your Loved Ones** *by Harvey J. Platt Attorney-at-Law* (softcover, 6 × 9,
256 pages, $14.95)

Licensing Art & Design, Revised Edition *by Caryn R. Leland*
(softcover, 6 × 9, 128 pages, $16.95)

**The Internet Publicity Guide: How to Maximize Your Marketing and Promotion
in Cyberspace** *by V. A. Shiva* (softcover, 6 × 9, 208 pages, $18.95)

Please write to request our free catalog. To order by credit card, call 1-800-491-
2808 or send a check or money order to Allworth Press, 10 East 23rd Street, Suite
210, New York, NY 10010. Include $5 for shipping and handling for the first book
ordered and $1 for each additional book or $10 plus $1 for each additional book if
ordering from Canada. New York State residents must add sales tax.

If you would like to see our complete catalog on the World Wide Web, you can find
us at ***www.allworth.com***